Sheepdogs at Work

To Willie Hainey, one of the best shepherds in Scotland, and his wife Isobel, one of the best cooks.

Sheepdogs at Work

**One Man and his dogs
by Tony Iley**

DALESMAN BOOKS
1982

THE DALESMAN PUBLISHING COMPANY LTD.,
CLAPHAM, via Lancaster LA2 8EB

First Published 1978

Reprinted 1979, 1982

© Tony Iley, 1978, 1982

ISBN: O 85206 439 X

Printed in Great Britain by
GEO TODD & SON,
Marlborough Street, Whitehaven.

CONTENTS

Photographs in the text are on pages 25 - 32 and 49 - 56.

The back cover photograph shows the author with Jace and pups Jay and Kip.

I've seen the Rocky mountains
And the Gulf of Mexico,
The California surfers
And palm trees by the row.

I've read the works of Shakespeare
And seen Piccasso's paint,
The sounds of concert pianists
And heard the bagpipes quaint.

And all of these have thrilled me,
But not one could compare
With watching collies working
A single or a pair.

There's magic in each movement
That Mozart never had,
And beauty in each turn
That makes my heart feel glad.

There's science in each answer
Of every whistled tone,
That Newton never thought of
Nor ever was he shown.

There's feeling in the handling
That only poets know,
Or men that work with sheepdogs
And feel the teamwork grow.

Wherever life may take you
In sunshine or in fog,
You'll never quite forget it
When once you've worked a dog.

CHAPTER I

THE DEVELOPMENT OF THE WORKING DOG

ONE OF the wonders of the world is to see a good Border Collie working in harmony with his master. Science and art are so closely combined as to make them inseparable. Each purposeful movement of the dog stems from instinctive knowledge and skilful training. The control of the sheep by the dog and the close knit partnership between dog and man cannot fail to move even the casual observer. The enthusiast, however, will not be content merely to observe. He will want to probe deeper into the phenomenon of the working dog. In order to gain a deeper understanding it is necessary to trace the development of the dog from pre-domesticated times right through to the present day.

An animal called Tomarctus, which lived about fifteen million years ago, is generally given credit for being the forerunner of all true dogs. From Tomarctus evolved various species of wolves, foxes and jackals. There is some uncertainty as to how our domesticated dogs emerged, but it is fairly certain that they carry both jackal and wolf blood. The difference in character between the predominantly wolf-blooded dog and the predominantly jackal-blooded dog is quite distinctive. The wolf-blooded dogs include the Husky and the Chow. The jackal-blooded dogs include most of the common present day breeds, the Alsatian and the sheepdog for example.

Konrad Lorenz, one of the greatest and most respected authorities on animal behaviour, writes: "The dependence of a dog on its master has two quite distinct origins. One is largely due to a life long maintenance of the ties which bind the young wild dog to its mother—and the other root of fidelity arises from the pack loyalty which binds the wild dog to the pack leader and other members of the pack". The latter root is more pronounced in the wolf-blooded dogs which, in attack, relied on absolute and selfless loyalty for survival. In the sheepdog and other predominantly jackal-blooded dogs the harmony with its master has its root in its dependence on the mother animal. Thus we must take care not to allow an excess of this childishness to persist into adulthood. If it does, the dog cringes painfully at the slightest hint of anger in its master's voice. It rolls on its back and produces a trickle of urine, a typically submissive gesture normally displayed by pups up to the age of six months. The opposite behaviour is equally undesirable. In this case the dog "calls no man master", and develops into a vagabond and delinquent. The "true" dog should hold a suitable place between these two extremes. To a large extent its position is determined by its genetic make up, but a pup can be moulded to quite a considerable degree by knowledgeable contact from puppy-hood.

7

The first association between canines and man probably occurred in the form of packs of jackals following the camps of nomadic man in order to scavenge. The jackals surrounding the camps would also be useful in warning the community of the approach of marauders by their barking. No doubt at some stage jackal pups were brought into the camp by children. These pups would eventually join in the hunts to receive a share of entrails. In this way the first step towards domestication was taken. From this time until somewhere around 1000 A.D. the dog became the constant companion of man, and a degree of specialisation within the species emerged. The early shepherds in Britain were accompanied by the predominantly jackal-blooded forerunners of the present day sheepdog. Their task at this time did not include working sheep: they were concerned with guarding them against thieves and predatory animals, mainly the wolf. The shepherds found it necessary to increase the size and viciousness of their dogs. As a result of this some of them tied their bitches deep in the forest whilst they were in season. The resulting progeny — half wolf and half shepherd's dog — were larger, stronger and more self-willed than their dams, and proved superior in their ability to face the wolves. Others, however, carried a surfeit of wolf traits and took to a life of sheep worrying. These were more easily dealt with than the full wolf and were usually culled by the shepherd and his dogs.

Thus over the next two centuries a fairly specialised kind of shepherd's dog became more of a fixed type. In those days, according to Tristam, the dogs were used "only for guarding not for working, but, when the wolves disappeared from England, the dogs developed less in size and became more intelligent but some of the savagery remained". As a result of this, the predominantly jackal-blooded dog gained popularity because of its more tractable nature. However, the former infusion of wolf blood contributed in some way to fixing the character of these early dogs.

According to Dr. Caius in his *Treatise of Englishe Dogges* in 1550, "Our shepherd's dog is not huge, vaste and big; but of indifferent stature because it has not to deal with the wolf since there be non in England". Perhaps most important of all he makes the first reference to the working of sheep as opposed to guarding them: ". . . this dog, either at the hearing of his master's voice or at his shrill and hoarse whistling and hissing or the wagging of his fist bringeth the wandering whethers and straying sheep into the self same place where his master's will and work is to have them". Again we must exercise our imagination to fill the gap between the first mentioned guarding dogs and the working dogs referred to by Dr. Caius. The dogs during this transitional period would be under the constant threat of the death penalty if they killed or mauled a sheep in any way. Even so, as the shepherds waved their arms, whistled and shouted to get the sheep into the folds, the dogs would vent their pent up hunting instinct by running up and down excitedly and barking behind the shepherd and his flock. The shepherd, quick to see how anxious the sheep were to get into the fold at this running and barking performance, would encourage it amongst his dogs. Thus, through generations of primitive but fairly effective and selective breeding, several isolated families of shepherds evolved a type of dog which tended to work as we know it. Crosses between dogs belonging to various families, combined with a certain degree of planned and unplanned inbreeding, fixed this working trait in the dogs.

Around 1600, Aldrobandus describes the "farm dog" thus: " In build he resembles a hound: he ought to be gentle to his own household, savage to those outside it, and not to be taken in by caresses. He should be robust with a muscular body and noisy in his deep bark, so that by his bold baying he may threaten on all sides and frighten away prowlers. He should have a fierce light in his eyes, portending the lightening attack of his teeth on the rash enemy. He should be black in his coat in order to appear more fearful to thieves in the daylight and being the same shade as night itself, to be able to make his way quite unseen by the enemies and thieves."

In approximately 1790 the presence of "eye" was recorded by James Hogg, the Ettrick shepherd-poet. He refers to it in a matter of fact way without surprise, leading us to believe that it was not a new innovation. He tells us the story about his favourite dog, Hector. Hogg had put some sheep in the pens late one night and then returned home. On his arrival at home Hector could not be found nor encouraged to come by his master's calling. Next morning, ". . . accordingly we (Hogg and his father) went together to the fold to turn out the lambs and there was poor Hector, sitting trembling in the very middle of the flake (wooden gate) that closed it with his eyes still fixed steadfastly on the lambs . . ." Again referring to Hector, ". . . he had a mortal antipathy for the family mouser, which was ingrained in his nature from puppyhood . . . whenever he was within doors his whole occupation was watching and pointing the cat from morning to night. When she flitted from one place to another so did he in a moment; then squatting down he kept his point sedulously till he was either called off or fell asleep".

James Scott of Overhall, Hawick (International Champion 1908 and 1909), said that he had not seen "eye" in dogs until 1875, when he saw it in a bitch owned by John Crozier, a herd at Teviot Water, who got her from Northumberland. Because of this it can be concluded that "eye" developed in various isolated families of dogs in the period between 1740 and 1870. At this time it would not be widespread, and its value would not be fully realised until the early trials began, starting with the first trial at Bala in Merioneth, Wales, in 1873. James Scott also remarks that dogs were harder to stop in those days (1880 approx.). However, in 1883, W. Wallace at Hawick trial amazed everyone by stopping them with a mere hiss or a low whistle and his quiet

9

manner of working dogs. Doubtless, the separate and relatively simultaneous appearance of "eye" would have developed in the Border area. The reason that this area produced the phenomenon and its own type of dog was one of necessity. Here the finer art of handling would develop. In the Highlands the barking type of dog which hunted in the rocks and bracken would be favoured. The same type would also be favoured farther south in England where the heavier, stiffer sheep would respond better to it.

Perhaps the other important landmark in the development of the present day working dog was in 1894. A Border farmed named Adam Telfer from Morpeth in Northumberland mated his own Roy, a very free eyed and frank expressioned dog, with his bitch Meg. She was a shy and self-conscious bitch and in September of that year she produced a litter of pups which included the black and white medium coated Old Hemp. Before Hemp died in 1901 he had sired over 200 pups. Hemp was apparently an excellent dog who rarely lay down and whose eyes blazed when he worked. Partly because of his excellence, and partly because of the development of roads, railways, sheep sales and trials, Hemp's fame spread, and he became one of the mainsprings in the foundation of the type of working collie that we now know. From the time of Hemp very little speculation is involved in the development of the breed as the International Sheepdog Society stud books provide a comprehensive and fairly reliable record right up to the present time.

CHAPTER II

THE PUP AND ITS EARLY TRAINING

IT almost goes without saying that one must see a pup before buying it. In this way many disappointments will be avoided. It is worth putting yourself to some trouble to select and collect the pup directly from the breeder, especially if he is not known to you. There is nothing more disappointing than to go to the station and collect an ill-thriven, pot-bellied, lousy pup. It will take considerable time, effort and money to build it up to the condition that it should have been in on arrival. Having gone to the trouble of inspecting the pup before committing yourself to the purchase, which one do you choose? It is almost impossible to select the pup that will turn out to be the best of the litter, but the odds can be weighed quite heavily in your favour by a strict selective process and a little thought. If the litter has been badly reared in any way, it is better not to allow yourself to become interested in them, as there is no shortage of healthy pups of most blood lines. Don't be palmed off with any pup that is inferior in any way, or you will have stepped on the road to disappointment.

The pup should be free from parasites, both internal and external. Infestation by parasites can usually be dealt with fairly easily, but why risk taking them into your own kennels? Often a dandruffy skin condition is seen in pups and this can be caused by lice that are too small for the naked eye to detect. If the pup with an unhealthy skin transmits its complaint into your own kennels, you will certainly find that the trouble involved in getting rid of it does not justify the purchase of the animal. The pup should neither be undershot nor overshot and his teeth should be white, well set and needle sharp. The bones should be strong and in proportion, and no sign of rickets should be present in any of the litter. Pay particular attention to the feet, as a pup that is badly splay-footed will hardly ever right itself, and it will be handicapped to some extent for the rest of its life.

If all things about the litter meet with your approval, the next stage is the actual selection of the pup. Often a pup in the litter will "speak" to you; pick this one every time. Although it may be nothing that you can put your finger on at the time, this certain thing that is transmitted to you by a particular pup will be an excellent basis for a growth of the vital bond between it and you. If no particular pup takes your eye, the biggest, boldest and happiest one is usually the best bet. Its temperament will probably be right. Avoid the pup that scurries to the back of the pen and refuses to play. It may easily have a bad temperament or need too much coaxing in its work and training to give the handler much satisfaction. The colour, too, is of some importance even if only marginally. Sheep, I am told, tend to become indifferent to a white dog and tend to be afraid of a completely black one. Sheep do not like shadows — a black dog moving about behind them is rather shadow-like and has a disturbing effect on them. Traditionally, the black and white dog is believed to be the best. All other things about the pup being to my satisfaction, I would hardly be swayed against it because of the colour except perhaps in the case of the white or almost white dog. This is merely a question of taste and, providing that the prospective buyer does not actually dislike the colour of the pup, there should be little difficulty. If you do not like its appearance, this may tend to start you off on the wrong foot. This must not happen at any cost. Once the dog has sensed any kind of permanent enmity between you, it will never give its best and you would be better off without it. Bad relationships tend to deteriorate rather than improve.

Presumably someone has somewhere bought a white pup full of worms and skin parasites, undershot, splay-footed and so nervous that it took half an hour to catch, but which afterwards turned out to be a topper. There is no doubt, however, that 99 per cent of such pups make no more than yard dogs. As we are only talking about weighing odds in our favour, there is no justification for becoming involved with unsound or unsatisfactory pups. There will be very little price difference between those which are excellent and well reared and those that are second rate pups, so the financial angle does not enter into it. Having selected a pup, you certainly intend to expend a great deal of time and hard effort on its education, hence the importance of starting off with the right material. You must be happy with the pup in every way before you buy it or you may never be happy afterwards.

There are exceptions to the rule of course. When Jace had three pups by Gillespie's Spot, the choice was very limited. The big dog pup had to go back in lieu of the service fee, and this left a tiny dog pup and a bitch pup. The tiny dog pup did not appeal to me at all, and in fact met an untimely end when it was attacked by a ferret. However, poetic justice prevailed and, a short time after the offence, the ferret met an equally untimely death. The bitch pup became my Hobson's choice. Bonnie always looked like a drowned rat. When I returned from the hill she met me at the garden gate, looking as if she had been dragged backwards through a weed-infested pond. Her appetite was poor and she was thin and scrawny. I despaired and hoped that someone would come and buy her—I even thought of giving her away for luck when someone bought another dog from me. However, no opportunity arose, and I eventually came to love the sight of this ragged pup wagging its tail at me as I approached the garden gate. At twelve weeks old she went to work—she was dynamite! Not even the old tups questioned her authority more than once. And so, from such an unpromising beginning Bonnie became a firm favourite.

Several years ago educational researchers took a look at children who had been brought up in orphanages. It was found that these children did not develop as well mentally or physically as those brought up in the family environment. This was quite a surprise finding for the researchers. The orphanage children often lived in more hygienic and better supervised conditions than the others. The deduction the researchers made was that the only factors which could account for this difference were early individual handling, love and attention, things that the orphanage children were deprived of to some extent. To test their theory the researchers set up a number of experiments with monkeys. Some were reared by artificial mothers, some without any kind of mother but in excellent conditions, and the third group was reared normally. The results of these experiments proved the importance of very early individual handling and affection in normal development.

These theories have never been tested on dogs, but if they were I am sure that early handling and affection by humans would be proved necessary for the bond between a dog and a human to develop to its full potential. Most people have seen a litter of pups that have scattered and hid when a stranger or even the breeder went into their pen. What a difference between them and the pups that run to anyone, tails wagging and intent on play. These pups, having had a good start, will be forever easier and more pleasurable to work with than those that are shy and nervous. For this reason it is of the utmost importance that the breeder spends as much time as he can handling and playing with the pups—I would go as far as to say that handling from the age of four or five days would be most beneficial. These pups will then contain the seeds which should germinate into the "true dog" through knowledgeable moulding.

The next important thing about a pup is the factor that most likely brought you to see the litter in the first place—the breeding. This is a matter of individual preference for the kind of dog which you think will get on best with you and your own particular style of handling. Remember that breeding can be a lottery as good, bad and indifferent pups may, without apparent reason, be produced from the same litter. Again, however, the odds can be weighed in your favour if you are prepared to be discriminative. Let us say that you have seen Glen working several times on different kinds of sheep and you are carried away with him. Bear in mind that by purchasing a Glen pup you will not be buying another Glen. The pup will be a combination of 50 per cent Glen and 50 per cent his mother. Not enough attention is paid to the bitch, a fact which never ceases to surprise me. There is very little to be said in favour of buying a pup from a breeding bitch that is kept exclusively for this purpose. She may be a non-worker, a bad worker, or of wrong temperament. Some of the pups may turn out to be good workers, if you are lucky. However, failure to follow a sound breeding or selection policy is a sizeable step on the road to nowhere. The undesirable traits of the bitch will appear once again along the line, even if not in the first generation. Take a pup from a good honest work bitch which is neither too fancy nor too rough. If she has proved herself on the trial field as well as in everyday work, so much the better, and, if she has demonstrated her ability to pass her qualities on to her offspring, again so much the better. At the present time it would also be an advantage for the pup to be bred from parents that have both passed the eye test for progressive retinal atrophy. The best plan, of course, when buying a pup is to see the results of an earlier mating of the same parents if this is possible. Remember that some crosses may produce good dogs but poorer bitches or vice versa.

Always look twice at the dog or bitch whose progeny you are interested in buying. Do not be led up the garden path by clever handling. Look deeply at the dog and decide if it is a "true dog" or merely a manufactured replica. First and foremost, its temperament must be right or it will certainly pass a similar temperament on to many of its offspring. If it is right the pup will be trainable, and you will be able to cure most of its faults fairly easily. If it is wrong the dog may refuse to be worked with, and an otherwise excellent animal may be wasted because of a single fault that the dog will not allow you to straighten out.

Of dogs which I have come to know quite well, a particular one which impressed me with its excellence of temperament was Jock Richardson's Sweep, a former International Driving Champion and Scottish Shepherd's Champion. On one particular winter weekend that Jock and I spent in the Rossendale Valley at the home of Jim Cropper, I saw a great deal of Sweep. He was a large black dog as big as an Alsatian, and he greeted everyone as a friend. His whole facial expression when you called him was one of enquiring good nature and, if dogs could shake you by the hand, Sweep would certainly have done so vigorously. This also proves the theory that dogs take after their master. Even as I write this passage I have a clear picture in my mind of Jock Richardson working Mirk on the hillside opposite Jim's farm, at the same time shedding sheep at his feet with Sweep and balancing a half full glass of whisky in his hand. Sweep was unperturbed by Mirk's commands, and nothing could distract his attention from his own particular task. It was because of his temperament, combined with outstanding hill ability, that I chose to use Sweep on my bitch Jace.

This litter produced David Carlton's Tony who took the Shepherd's Aggregate trophy at the Lockerbie Internationals in 1976.* Tony was the biggest, boldest pup in the litter. After he was eight weeks old I never saw him again until I returned from Canada. By this time he was 15 months old, and David had just bought him for pup price. In a very short time he began to show signs of hidden potential. After a couple of months with David this potential was

*Tony also won the English heat on the BBC2 series, "One Man and his dog."

realised and he was well on the way to becoming an outstanding worker. But the best laid schemes of mice and men often "gang agley", as Burns reminds us. Suddenly Tony went lame and his pads became raw sores. The local witch-doctors were consulted but no cure was forthcoming. For months it seemed that Tony would never do any serious work again. Happily, after a brief stay at the Royal Dick Veterinary Hospital in Edinburgh, he returned to active duty and competition. The root of the problem turned out to be an allergy to hookworm. Tony's mother, Jace, incidentally, although the smallest in a litter of Tot Longton's Gyp and Bosworth Coon was one of those pups which spoke to me as soon as I saw her.

Going back to an earlier statement, the reason that I initially ordered a pup of this breding was the fact that I had been impressed by Tot's Jed, a bitch of the same breeding from an earlier litter. The day that I collected Jace from Lee End, Tot ran Jed for me, and I saw a true dog. Every move by Jed caused a response in the sheep; there was no unnecessary work done by her, no fuss, no noise, nothing fancy, just a sound workmanlike display. She was obviously well handled by Tot, but even on my long journey up to Scotland, when I looked closely and deeper at what I had seen, I knew she was a true dog.

To get back to the pup, enough has been said on what is required in it to give the reader a good idea of my opinion on the subject. Thus, having gone to all the trouble of selecting and collecting the pup, it would be foolhardy to neglect the distemper and hardpad injection. Having got the pup home safely (try not to feed it immediately before the journey), install it in warm draught-proof quarters and give it food and water. From now on it is entirely dependent on you. Its feeding is merely a matter of common sense—it cannot be expected to thrive on one or two meals a day at this stage. I like to throw a whole dead rabbit to the pup as a supplement to its meals. In this way, it can help itself to the meat, bone and innards. The rabbit's stomach also contains greens, which will help to keep the dog's skin in good condition. It is also good for the pup to exercise itself by tearing and ripping at the carcase.

The first and very important stage in the pup's education consists of the vital early lessons. It is surprising how many people neglect these and dismiss them as unimportant — apparently they have nothing to do with working sheep. It is totally wrong to keep the pup tied in a building till it is seven or eight months old and then bring it out into the world and expect it to know all the things that are taken for granted in the older dog. Not knowing its name, it will no doubt take advantage of its new found freedom and refuse to come back when you call it. The exasperated handler then has to resort to chasing and capturing the pup. By this procedure he begins by alienating himself from the animal and thus starting off on the wrong foot. It will almost certainly run around aimlessly and be half frightened to death at the sound of a tractor, the bucket that it knocks over and the first sight of a cow. The pup must grow up with as wide an experience of the world as possible. From a very early age it should be encouraged to follow its master about and take its surroundings for granted—in this way they offer no distraction when it begins work. This applies not only to the pup but also to the older dog. A dog which is at one with its surroundings is firm and unflappable.

The most unflappable dog I have ever owned was Shen. She was my first dog and went everywhere with me. One year I gave a demonstration with her at a local agricultural show, using the main ring which was set up for show jumping. Shen had to get the sheep from a trailer to the main ring and this was the most difficult part of the whole operation. The crowd refused to part, cars almost drove over me, riders on horses attempted to trample us into the dust and the brass band played on. Shen never batted an eyelid. I still have a vivid recollection of her working the sheep right through a horse's legs. Children tried to stroke her, hooligans were whistling at her, and drivers were revving their engines all around us. Shen didn't even notice them. The demonstration went so well that we were asked back the following year. On this occasion I had borrowed some ewes that had only seen a dog on rare occasions. They were newly clipped and it was a roasting hot day. I steered them very gently round the course, but just as they were about to pop into the pen one sheep dropped stone dead. For an instant I could have crawled into a worm hole. The crowd, however, thought she had just laid down to be awkward and raised a great laugh. They were even more amused when I lifted her into the pen (taking care to set her in a realistic pose) and then penned the rest of the sheep. I think some of them were beginning to wonder when I also carried her out! The following year I was not asked to demonstrate.

Several years ago I was standing at a trial with Harry Huddleston watching a "hot dog" running riot round the course. Later on the handler of this dog came over to us and remarked that it was needing plenty of work to steady it down. Harry replied that work would not steady her down as much as trailing it about would, a statement that seemed almost irrelevant to me at the time, but, as I began to acquire a better understanding of the working dog, the force and truth of that remark became apparent. My friend and one time neighbouring herd, Willie Hainey, discovered the value of this trailing about when he was a "single herd" and was allowed to keep just two dogs. Some of the dogs that he broke were bought from dairy farmers whom he met in the days of driving hoggs in Ayrshire. These young dogs had invariably spent their lives tied up in a byre, and anything could happen when they were unchained. Eventually he changed his system. He would buy a pup and send it home to his mother to rear until it was eight or ten months old. "These young dogs were half broken before you started to break them", he commented. As a result of this, very little pressure was needed in the breaking and this proved most valuable. The less you have to pressure a young dog during the early lessons with sheep, the better you will get on together in both the short and long terms. It is therefore important that the pup's education begins as soon as you get it home. If you are fortunately situated, the pup may have almost complete freedom until it is so keen that it cannot resist going to sheep to have a go on its own. All this is impossible if the handler has got quite a few pups and young dogs about him at the same time, but the solution to this will lie in his own hands.

To diverge into theory, the early education of pups and children should follow a similar pattern. Perhaps one of the greatest educational thinkers was Jean Jacques Rousseau, whose ideas had a great effect on primary education in the whole of Europe. In his book *Emile* he describes how he would educate a child—Emile—if he had the time and money to devote himself entirely to this task. Much of this could be applied to the pup with advantage. His main theory was that the child, or pup in our case, should not be constantly restrained by a set of dos and don'ts. Within reason let it learn for itself by experience; these lessons are always the best learned and longest lasting. For instance, let if find out that to get under the wheel of a wheelbarrow is an unpleasant experience. It will apply this lesson to cars, tractors, etc., and perhaps avert a far more serious accident later on. This, of course, does not mean that you should try to run over it with a barrow-load of dung. However, when the barrow is empty, do not go out of your way to avoid the pup, or it will expect all vehicles to act in the same manner. Let it find out that, if it strays far from you in a strange place, it gets lost for a while. This lesson can easily be arranged a few fields distant from home, when you will obviously be keeping a watchful eye on it from behind a wall. The lesson learned, the pup will soon know that it must stay close to you in a strange place or when you call its name. Let it learn to cross a stream, climb a low wall, ride in a car, and see the various types of livestock.

A pup, like a child, draws its reaction from yours. If, for example, a gun goes off with a loud bang and you panic to get hold of the pup for fear that it will run away, it will soon learn to panic and run at the sound of a gun. Rather carry on as before without showing any emotion. The pup will be startled on the first few occasions, but your own indifference will communicate to it and it too will grow indifferent. Let it sit at your feet by a busy cross-roads and learn that fast moving traffic is no reason for panic, merely for a level-headed wide berth. Because the pup draws all its reactions to strange things from your own, you must take great care never to do anything suddenly panicky or even excessively hurriedly.

This brings to mind an early lesson that I learned from that excellent and polished handler, Jock Richardson. It was about the time that Jace was seven months old. I had been running her in Jock's field and, after the various dogs had had their turn, we set off back for the house. All the dogs were running about playing together and I had not noticed Jace slip away from the others and gather the ten hoggs up to the fence. Not being able to get them through the wire she was dogging them up to it frantically. As soon as I saw what was happening I began to shout excitedly, "That'll do, that'll do". Being young and keen, Jace dodged them against the fence even harder. I set off at a run to get her, but before I had strode four paces Jock's mighty voice boomed out my name. I stopped as if struck by lightning (I now know why all his dogs stop so well) and turned to look at Jock. "Don't hurry", he said in a quiet calm voice. I walked a few more paces and said in an equally calm voice, "That'll do." Jace looked up at me and left the sheep like a well-trained old dog.

In the early training of a pup, willingness to come when called and to lie down at command is a rudimentary essential. The two lessons are easily combined into one, which make it easier on both pup and trainer. Teach the pup to lie down by pushing it firmly but gently to the ground at the command. When it has mastered this, it can be taught to remain there until you have retreated a few paces and called it back to you. The pup naturally wants to come to you during the lesson, so when you call its name it will be only too pleased to do so. Be free with praise; it is at least as effective as punishment. Praise will also serve to strengthen the bond between dog and master. The training of a young dog should be a positive pleasure to both dog and man. If you go out for a training session with the intention of finding fault with the dog rather than finding virtue, these sessions will soon become a chore to you and hateful to the dog. It is as well to keep this constantly in mind by getting "mentally set" yourself before unclipping the pup for a turn with the sheep. Obviously the faults have to be cured—but not to the exclusion of everything else. If the pup's nature is sound and the handler's attitude right, most faults can be cured without going into the field determined to put them right at all costs. Never try determinedly to cure a fault at the expense of interfering with the young dog's natural desire to work, or you will end up wishing you had let the fault go unchecked.

Regarding the age at which to start these training sessions, I like to start the "lying down and coming to hand" lessons between eight and ten weeks old. These must always be kept short—five minutes at a time is sufficient. People often complain ". . . but I haven't had time to bother with it". If any man has not got five minutes to spare twice of three times a day, he should either change his job or sell his dogs, because he certainly will not have time to break them during the later stages.

About this time also contrary to the opinion of many handlers better than myself, I cannot resist taking the pup to sheep. The first two or three times it shows only inquisitiveness, but this soon develops into a definite interest and a firm desire to work. I like to get about ten quiet hoggs in a small field and work them at hand with an experienced dog. The pup at first wants to stay by my feet but eventually shows signs that it wants to chase as the old dog causes a movement in the sheep. I encourage the pup to gather by putting myself at twelve o'clock to it. At the same time I use the old dog behind me to keep the sheep from breaking away and the pup losing them. By the time the pup is four or five months old, even though it is not fast enough to pass sheep, it can be quite proficient at this game of holding them up to you. This will be partly by its own efforts and partly by yours. The experienced dog is still used to prevent any serious breaks. Gradually, more of the responsibility for "holding up" falls on the pup and less on the trainer. The trainer can then begin to walk backwards, constantly changing his direction, letting the pup bring the sheep to him and helping it when required. It can now be stopped and started easily, and it enjoys its work. Never chase after it to catch it at the end of the ten minute lesson. Ask it to lie down and make it stay, as learned in a previous lesson. Now slowly walk around the sheep towards it, allowing them to drift away. When they have moved twenty or thirty yards away, say "that'll do" and walk out of the field. The pup will probably run after them but will not be able to catch them with its limited size and speed. Finding that it is alone in the middle of the field with its master disappearing through the gate it will remember its earlier "getting lost" lesson and quickly run to join him. Congratulate it heartily all the way to the drinking bowl of which it will be very glad. If at any time during the short training sessions the pup's attention begins to wane, finish immediately. He must be made to feel that he is permitted to do these lessons and not obliged to do them.

At this stage the experienced eye can make a fairly accurate assessment of the pup's future potential. Latent faults and tendencies can often be sensed before they appear and in this way they can be helped, if not entirely cured, before they are fully developed. For instance, if a shortage of power is suspected, the pup will hardly ever be given the lie down command on sheep. It will be encouraged to keep coming and to stop on its feet, if it must stop. It will also be encouraged to flank tightly and go out very narrowly, otherwise the shortage of power when it is fully apparent will be a greater handicap. If the pup is going to develop into a strong, hard-to-handle dog, insist more on the lie down. In this position he will not be able to steal ground and he can be taught to stop on his feet at a later date. Encourage him to flank rather wider than is necessary. In this way, when he matures and his flanks tighten a little, he will be just about right.

Having spoken about teaching the dog to flank tight or wide, it will be necessary to explain how this is done without pressure on either dog or handler. Firstly, the wide flank. Manoeuvre till you obtain the position shown on the diagram with the dog at twelve o'clock to the handler. When the young dog is stopped, sheep settled and handler

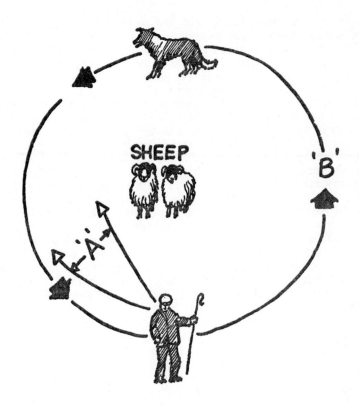

calm, ask it to flank to the right. At the same time begin to walk towards it, i.e. to your left. Its instinct will obviously be to flank to the left to hold the sheep to you. Calmly stop it and ask it again in an unhurried natural voice to flank to its right. Eventually the young dog will grasp the idea that it must run to its right, behind you and completely round the sheep to head them once more. When it has learned this, the handler can walk towards it at an increasing distance from the sheep before asking it to flank behind him. By altering the distance "A", the width of the flank can be controlled. During the later stage it is better to stop the dog at position "B", where its flank begins to tighten on to the sheep again.

Conversely, to encourage the dog to flank tightly, flank it on to the sheep instead of off them. Here the dog is not flanked behind the handler. As the handler moves away from the sheep and to his right, the dog automatically moves towards the sheep and to its right. At the same time the right hand whistle or command is given rather more sharply. This sharpness will encourage the dog to flank more tightly. Before the initial flanking lessons the young dog should already be familiar with the whistles—although it won't know them. They should have been given during the earlier wearing sessions. Here, however, no attempt should have been made to make the pup move either way to a whistle. If it already wanted to go in a certain direction during the natural course of wearing, the appropriate whistle should have been given at the same time.

In the course of these early lessons much work and frustration can be saved by giving each pupil a great deal of individual attention and thought. It is a good plan to spend ten minutes in the armchair studying the pup for every five minutes spent in the field working it. Bend to fit every individual circumstance and be prepared to take advantage of the unexpected, even if it is contrary to the rules. No pup should be dominated with an iron hand or subjected to the use of a stick to enforce discipline. The stick is the dog handler's worst enemy, although often he cannot realise it. "Leave the stick at home when breaking a young dog", someone once said to me. "If dogs could be made by the use of a stick there would be plenty of good dogs about". The best results are invariably obtained through patience and building the bond of confidence between man and dog. After these lessons have been repeated several times, the pup will begin to antici- pate what you are about to ask it to do. When this happens, it is a good plan to ask it to do the unexpected. This will have the effect of making the pup listen to what you are asking it to do rather than going through the same routine performance every session.

By now the pup will be about eight months old. As a result of good feeding and plenty of exercise it will have grown sufficiently to have the speed to pass the hoggs on which it has been training. At this time the first outrun lessons can be given. The pup will be keen to go, and this keenness should not be dampened down by. discipline rigorously enforced. Let the sheep settle down thirty yards away and stand with the pup about ten yards to the left or right of you. Before giving the appropriate whistle in a quiet, steady manner, make sure that the pup has seen the sheep and knows where it has to go. Do not wave your arms about or try to chase the pup out. Apart from being totally unnecessary this will only divert its attention from the sheep to you. If you start to chase the pup up the field to keep it out on its outrun, you will soon realise, and even worse it will realise, that it can beat you to the sheep every time. This realisation will be something of a revelation to the pup, which up to now has regarded you as a master and superior being as well as a friend. As a general rule, try not to give an order unless you are in a position to see that it is carried out. Otherwise the pup will recognise your limitations and begin to take advantage of you. At this stage do not worry too much if the pup splits the sheep, comes too tight or even crosses its course so long as it gets to the back of the sheep without stalking or eyeing them. In a way it is a time of desperation. Let it get to the back of the sheep, regardless of how it gets there. Allowing it to cross its course or come too tight sounds foolhardy advice, but remember that when it is properly broken it will never think of doing these things. Because a young baby hits his father over the head with a rattle does not mean that he will make this a habit, using an axe as he gets older. Many dogs go out badly as a result of being made to go out perfectly as young dogs. Unless a dog is desperately keen to get behind sheep at this stage, by the time it is broken it may go out in a slack or indifferent manner. By giving some thought to the setting up of sheep and dog with regard to the lie of the land, it can be engineered so that it is almost impossible for a dog to cross over or go seriously wrong on its outrun. A pup which shows signs of natural cast should never be chased out, or its outrun will certainly finish up far too wide when the dog is broken. If a hint of cast is seen, that is acceptable enough, let it develop naturally and without any pressure.

By the time the pup is 10 or 11 months old it may be capable of gathering sheep at fifty or a hundred yards in a determined if somewhat hasty way. It will stop quickly at the whistle and flank with the drift of the sheep as it brings them to you, and will have the idea of gathering fixed firmly in its mind. As it reaches your feet with the sheep, they can be turned on to a drive as it is done at a trial. The pup should be encouraged to drive just for a few yards before calling it off and walking to the other end of the field for the next gather. The pup that has been taught to flank behind the handler may not want to flank in front of him when it begins to drive. If this is the case, when you turn the sheep initially, take a few steps backwards so that you are up against a wall or fence. In this way the pup will have to flank in front of you. Providing that the idea of driving begins to "click" with the pup, ask it to do so as you walk along beside it and increase the distance that you fall behind it each day. It is usually about this time that the pup begins to differentiate between the left and right whistle as you ask it to take them on the drive. It now has no guide to the direction that the sheep should be taking except by listening to and differentiating between the whistles. It is a thing that seems to come to the pup all of a sudden. One day it does not know them and the next day it is about 75 per cent right in its choice of direction. By the end of the week it is 99 per cent sure of them but may occasionally refuse to answer correctly. It will be an advantage, when teaching the pup to drive, to alternate between allowing it to head the sheep to bring them back and calling it off at the end of the drive. This degree of uncertainty in the pup will help to keep it keen on the drive. If it is always brought back to the handler at the end, it will start looking back and waiting to be called off, which is undesirable. Even at this stage the duration of the lessons should not exceed ten minutes or so. Once a day will be sufficient. However, twice or three times a day would certainly be better and will not have the effect of jading the dog.

22

The last two of the early lessons can be given at this stage, and these will be the blow back and shed. Again by doing things naturally and by making full use of the circumstances, these lessons can easily be combined into one. Begin the lesson with the shedding before the pup is tired and while it is still very keen to get the sheep. Make it lie down in the twelve o'clock position and divide the flock yourself. Then ask the pup to come to you. The shed may be missed altogether but it does not matter at the moment. Make the pup come right to your feet at the command and it will soon learn to do so. When it has come in to you, turn it on to the shed sheep. Put yourself at twelve o'clock to it and encourage it to wear sheep to you.

After wearing them for ten or fifteen seconds the other sheep will still be in the pup's mind. It will probably cast a look in their direction before long, especially if you ask it to lie down. As soon as you see this encourage it to gather them, giving the blow back whistle at the same time. These lessons are particularly enjoyed by a strong dog and it will become proficient in a remarkably short time. For this reason the shed, once learned, should not be practised too often or the dog will become shed happy and take the shed when it should be wearing at the pen. Here again, the dog must not be allowed to anticipate the blow back command after the shed or it will let you down when you want to hold the shed sheep. Occasionally the training session should finish with the shed sheep worn right away from the remaining sheep without the blow back given at all.

By the time the pup is 13 or 14 months old, it should be able to manage a small trial course in a rather determined if unpolished manner, and now its training as such should stop. Many traditional handlers may be horrified by the asking of so much from a pup so young. There is no cause for worry about this. At no time has pressure been exerted on the pup; its natural instincts have been encouraged and its desire to work has never taken second place to discipline. Personally I prefer the pup that takes the law into its own hands somewhat, as it will grow into a more powerful, confident dog that can use its own initiative. Whatever the circumstances it will always do something: the pup that shows a certain degree of stubbornness may finish up the better dog. The pup which is easily moulded may finish up far too fancy.

CHAPTER III

THE NEXT STAGE

I ONCE HEARD a conversation between two men at a trial, alluding to a certain man. One remarked that this man was going to send his dog to be trained by another respected handler. Jokingly the reply was that he should leave the dog at home and go himself. Like many other remarks made in jest, more truth than was intended lies therein. It is ourselves that we should concentrate on breaking, and the dogs will take care of themselves. The proof of this lies in any international catalogue; the dogs may change, but the men remain the same for 80 per cent of the time. It is our own attitude to the dog and its handling that is all-important, and this must be borne in mind from start to finish.

Our pup has now become a young dog virtually broken but with a great deal to learn and with many hundred mistakes ahead of it. These mistakes must be forgiven but not to the extent of letting them develop into faults or habitually recurring mistakes. The great maturer from now on is as much work as possible. Most herds and handlers tend to take the "old dog" to do the job and leave the young dog at home. The only time that this is excusable is when you may be in a desperate hurry. The other mortal sin which hinders the development of the dog is the handler having too many young pups about to be able to spend enough time with each. How many times has this excuse been given? I dread to think. The solution rests with the handler—do not have too many about. The situation can be If a further hundred are added all six hundred suffer, not just the likened to a sheep farm which can carry a stock of only 500 ewes. extra hundred. A fair idea of the number of dogs that a handler can keep well trained and in good order can be demonstrated by taking them all at once into the front room for the evening. If they cannot all be controlled without fuss, cut the number and spend the same amount of time educating them. If they scratch continually, are smelly and are generally unpleasant to sit with, again cut the number and spend the same time looking after those that remain.

As stated previously, training as such should now stop and the dog should be allowed to mature into the finished article through its work. Use as few commands as possible, as the dog will respond better to those that are given and enjoy the freedom of working. Allow the dog to use its initiative before resorting to a command in everyday work. The whistle must always be given clearly and without panic. When the dog is stopped, if the whistle is too sharp and abrupt, the

24

A proud father again! P. J. Connearn's Kim with a litter of future workers.

Two pups wait eagerly for their new owner to collect them and develop their full potential.

Well-reared pups survey the farm yard from their elevated position. One of them takes the first exploratory step down.

(M. V. Sutcliffe)

"So that's what the butler saw!"
(Farmers Guardian)

Lakeland shepherds' dogs on the slopes above Wasdale Head. These smooth-haired, leggy dogs are ideally adapted for working on the punishing Lakeland fells.

(Peter Dawson)

A wintry day on the Pennines. Len Greenwood's Kim watches intently
as the sheep tuck into their hay.

(Farmers Guardian)

A black and tan collie, W. Hardisty's Jim was the 1961 English
National Champion.

(Farmers Guardian)

"Come on then, get the gate open!" T. T. McKnight's Drift holds a
bunch of Scottish blackface ewes at his Canonbie farm.
(Terrence Leigh)

"Eye and style". The author's Jace in a classic pose.

" 'Scuse me, have you seen any sheep? "

"Eye to eye with eye". Shen holds a sheep motionless with her strong eye.

Chris Todd, a Lakeland shepherd, inspects some of his flock. His four sheepdogs are under complete control and ready for their next commands.

(Ivor Nicholas)

dog will tend to "dig in" to the ground too hard, and this will certainly upset the sheep, especially on a trial field. A steady, firm and unhurried whistle will cause the dog to sink nicely to the ground, and this will also help it to lift in a steadier manner. When sheep are lifted after the stop whistle, a drawn out lift whistle should be used. This was pointed out to me by Tot Longton, who helpfully made the valid criticism that I was not getting the best out of my dog because I was not letting it feel its sheep on the lift. The easier, more drawn out lift whistle made it feel the sheep better and so take charge of them in a far nicer way. Apart from this the dog now gets the chance to weigh up the sheep and adjust to them for the rest of the course if it is on a trial field. This ability does not come overnight and must be striven towards with the young dog.

The same principle applies to the flank whistles. I once had a young dog which persisted in flanking tightly. One afternoon I travelled the narrow road through the Trough of Bowland to Tim Longton's Rooten Brook farm to ask his advice. Tim pointed out that I was almost making the bitch flank tightly by giving it sharp panicky flank whistles. Within a very short time of taking care with her whistles she opened up on her flanks and outrun without any further interference whatever. Even at this stage of maturing the young dog, you must always be kidding it along. If you see the dog wanting to do something which will not be detrimental, ask it to do this very thing. In this way it will think it has done it because you asked it to do so. The attitude of being permitted to do rather than being obliged to do will also be perpetuated in this way. Again this will be a golden opportunity for the handler to praise the dog, and because of this it will revel in carrying out his orders. It is also a suitable time to finish the training session—always on a good note—so that the dog will eagerly await the next chance to go to the sheep and approach its work happily.

It never ceases to amaze me that a dog at a distance of half a mile on a hill can hear a whistle that might be completely drowned by the noise of a rolling bucket. This fact can be used to advantage on suitable days. The dog can be commanded with these almost silent whistles, and after a time you can almost feel it straining to catch them when it is in doubt. It will enjoy taking them when it does pick them up. As an extension of this quiet whistling technique, if you really want to impress the dog with the urgency of a certain command, a sharp loud whistle makes it jump to. This is the time when the dog should learn the various subtleties and intonations of the whistles. It should have a wide flank for a hollow drawn-out whistle and a tight quick one for a sharp desperate whistle, these together with all the various in-between shades. Only during its everyday work will it easily grasp and learn these finer points.

Up to this point I have given the impression that the commands are always by whistle. Indeed for the first ten years of my dog breaking, all my dogs except Shen were broken to the whistle only. I was never happy with the spoken command, but it is however very valuable. As the late J. M. Wilson said: "Whistled commands tend to make a dog hot". A pup, I think, understands a spoken command easier than it understands a whistled one. "J.M." used to tell us to spend time talking to our dogs—"But talk sense" he would say. Some people are more fortunate than others in having a good "doggy voice". Handlers who do not have such a voice should stick to whistled commands outby but could use the voice inby. One of the best ways to upset sheep is to whistle loudly in their ears, and this is just what many competitors do when they are working their dogs at the pen. A far better result would be produced by using an almost inaudible whistle or a quiet spoken command.

Up to now I have said nothing about punishment apart from decrying the use of the stick. The reader may possibly have branded me as an idealist or a theorist. I know only too well that on certain occasions the only way out is to punish the dog. If, however, the handler cannot count the number of times he has punished the broken dog in twelve months on one hand, he is using his strength to the exclusion of his brain. Sensitivity to punishment varies considerably with individual dogs, and this fact must be borne in mind before administering this deterrent. To quote Konrad Lorenz again. "Every form of canine punishment is effective less by virtue of the pain it causes than by the revelation of the power of the administrator". This profound and deep statement must really sink into the dog trainer and become a part of his attitude rather than just an idea with which he casually agrees. The most effective way to punish a dog, bearing this in mind, is to lift it off the ground with both hands grasping the sides of its neck, look it straight in the eye and threaten it with a quiet growling. This to the human seems a very mild punishment, but we must always take care never to impart human feelings, motives or understanding to the dog. This punishment appeals to the essence of the dog, as it is so similar to the reproof administered by the pack leader who is supremely dominant. A pack leader who could lift the offender's hind legs right off the ground to shake it would indeed be powerful enough to command respect and obedience. Furthermore, this form of punishment does not make the dog jumpy, edgy and hand shy as the use of the stick usually does. There is also a belief that man has a strange power in his eyes. In the realms of fiction Mowglie, of Rudyard Kipling's *Jungle Book,* was expelled from the wolf pack because they could not bear his gaze. As in many fictitious stories there is an element of truth in this. It is a fact that mammals rarely look at each other or at a trusted human directly eye to eye for long periods of time. This is mainly due to the structure of their eye. In man there is a central groove in the retina which is constructed so as to give us a clear vision of the point upon which we focus. The rest of the objects to the side or in the background are less distinct. In animals this central part of the retina is not so specialised, and it receives a fairly constant if less sharp vision of a larger area. Thus

34

dogs and other mammals very rarely fix their gaze on an object for more than a few seconds at a time. If an animal does fix its gaze, it usually means that it is afraid of that object or it intends to take drastic action against it. It could be said that the fixing of an animal's gaze is usually equivalent to taking aim. If then your gaze is fixed on the dog's eyes for a long time, this is interpreted as something hostile and malevolent. Herein lies the secret of the power of the human eye, which can be developed by the perceptive trainer. As an off-shoot of this idea, when trying to make friends with a shy dog never face him directly and stare into his eyes life a wolf about to make the kill. Rather look just to the side or above him and only let your eyes rest on his briefly and as if it were by accident. The purpose of punishment is to make the dog useful in a certain situation and not to alienate him from it. Therefore after punishing the dog your power will have been revealed to him, so now be immediately on good terms with him and make him do correctly the action for which you have punished him. On certain occasions, however, you may go from bad to worse by repeating the operation immediately. Rather than weakening the bond with the dog forget it for now, and try again in another week. I repeat, never enforce discipline at the expense of interfering with the dog's natural desire for work.

The topic of punishment always brings to my mind an occasion on which I almost administered the final deterrent to a dog. I had bought a big handsome dog of about two years old. When I got him he knew nothing at all, in fact he did not even have a name so I named him Jim after Jim Cropper whose great dog Fleet was his grandsire. Every time I let Jim off the lead he made straight away to sheep and had to be captured before he would leave them. This went on for two or three weeks without improvement. Eventually I could walk him at heel without the lead, until he saw sheep and then he was off again.

One hot summer's day, Jim was up to his usual tricks of refusing to come off his sheep. Every time I got near him he departed and gathered another field of sheep. It took a great deal of effort to repress feelings of violence towards him on that hot day. Eventually after almost three hours, and walking many a mile, I captured him. "Good dog", I said between gritted teeth. We walked away from the sheep; I was determined that Jim would walk the last quarter mile home, at heel and without the lead, no matter how long it took. I released him and we began walking home. Fifty yards from our objective, Jim raised his head, looked back in the direction of the sheep and set off. I have never run as fast in my life. He jumped the field wall. I caught up with him and grabbed him in mid-air as he was dropping down the other side of the wall. To my amazement he also grabbed me and began to worry me in earnest. In the struggle that followed I got hold of him round the throat and began to squeeze, not daring to let go, as he really meant business. About ten seconds later he fell limp in my hands. I let go and stood up above him. Soon

35

he staggered to his feet like a drunk. I said, in as natural a voice as I could muster, "That'll do Jim". I turned from him and set off for home and he followed obediently if somewhat shakily to his kennel. Jim never tried to leave me again until I asked him to go. He always came off his sheep at the first asking and soon became a very useful dog.

I had taken advantage of an unusual situation that had presented itself. To have punished Jim with a stick after capturing him when he would not come off his sheep would certainly have ruined him completely. Jim's fault seems to be a common one in dogs. Unfortunately it is one of the most difficult to cure because the dog does not seem to associate any punishment that you administer with the breaking away to sheep. Rather it associates it with the returning to its master, and so the situation often deteriorates. I have cured many dogs of this fault through patience alone. Always praise them when you finally capture them and you will eventually succeed.

Another sudden cure which was effected at the right moment and was connected with the same fault comes to mind. My wife, Marilyn, once bought a bitch called Tib. Every time she let Tib off the chain she made straight to the hill and worked sheep till captured. The situation continued every day for about a month without any improvement. If Marilyn had once lost her temper and used the stick on Tib all would have been lost. As usual Tib set off for the hill one day when she had been unchained and no amount of calling her back did any good. She eventually gathered up some sheep and was dogging them up to the wall at the sheep dipper. Marilyn arrived on the scene, jumped over the wall and caught Tib unawares. It was dipping time, so she lifted Tib straight into the full dipper. Tib was startled and shocked at the suddenness of these new tactics. The event imprinted itself so strongly on her mind that Tib never again went to the hill on her own.

At this stage in the dog's maturation I like to seek out what is difficult on the hill and ask the dog to do it. The dog should learn not to panic at your attempts to do the difficult. Soon the difficult will become easy and the impossible merely difficult. However, always know when to say "that'll do" and go to give the dog some help. The dog is to some extent like a blood horse and loses its ability to think when a certain point of excitement is reached. Towards the end of this stage the dog and man will have great confidence in each other and be able to communicate every slight intention and need. This confidence and communication is supremely important especially at trials. It is no good running a dog in which you have no confidence —it will let you down every time.

I often wonder if we give our dogs the chance to develop their full potential. It is amazing what can be done given the right circumstances. Recently an ancient volume called *Shepherds of Britain* came my way and many tales in it are quite beyond our ken. For example: "I was interested the other day in watching a flock of sheep, attended by a drover and his dog as they were passing along a turnpike road. The man went into an ale house by the road side, leaving the dog to look after the sheep. They spread themselves over the road, some lying down, others feeding, while the dog, faithful to his trust, watched carefully. When any carriage, or person was seen on the footpath, the dog gently drove the sheep to one side to make a passage, then resumed his station at the ale house door."

Also, the author tells us how he and his neighbour, both farming in Surrey, purchased 200 Cheviots "in the north" and employed a shepherd to drive them down. When he arrived, they asked him how he had fared. "Why, very badly", said the man, "for I had a young dog and he didn't manage well in keeping the sheep from running up lanes and out of the way places." The author continues : "The next year we had the same man and the same number of sheep. In answer to our question about his journey, he informed us that he had got on well, for his dog had recollected all the turnings off the road which the sheep had passed the previous year and kept them straight the whole way."

CHAPTER IV

TRIALS

MUCH criticism is often levelled against "professionals" at trials. Personally I admire professionalism in any walk of life. My utmost respect goes to teams of dogs and men who can go on to any field and work with sheep which vary from those as stubborn as mules to those as wild as deer. That these "professionals" can repeatedly and consistently count in the money surely deserves respect and admiration and should be a source of inspiration to the rest of us. At the same time we must remember that they are beatable, and we must direct our efforts to this end.

When competing at trials it is up to you and the dog. "Never play to the gallery", said Harvey Smith when talking about show jumping. This applies to dog running too. Showmanship is all very fine in the wrestling ring and on the stage, but there is no room for it on the trial field. Here both dog and handler must give their full attention to doing a sound workmanlike job efficiently. In spite of the shortcomings of our present day trials, the trial field is an ideal situation for comparing dogs and bringing to light the true dogs. This will serve as a useful aid to the breeder in his selection and planning. The true dog will usually be in control of the sheep despite the blunders of a bad handler or the misfortunes of the good handler. Even these true dogs, however, will have their faults. The secret is not to chase a mythical perfect dog with which to compete but to find a true dog whose few incurable faults or shortcomings you can put up with. The man who is able to tolerate a few faults will always have a dog to compete with; the man who cannot tolerate will never have one. It is better to find a dog with a lot of things about him that you like. Then, by skilfully working to eliminate the things you do not like, you will get the best out of him.

There are one or two elementary but often neglected rules to follow before the competitor actually goes to the post, the first of these being to let the dog empty himself before his run. The next point is equally important, and that is to learn the exact course. It is not the course director's or trial manager's job to seek you out and tell you the course. The onus lies on you to ask him. If it is at all possible to watch three or four runs from start to finish before competing, much can be learned. Sheep invariably tend to bear the same way on any particular section of the course and the same mistakes are often made by handler after handler. Finally, before you walk to the post to begin your run get "mentally set", i.e. determined not to panic at any cost and really mean business.

There is no place for slap-happy work on the trial field. I always deduct outrun points from any competitor setting his dog off while walking to the post. The post is there to start from, and indeed must be started from. The actual walking to the post, which is of more importance than many people think, should be in a direct line with the sheep. This gives the dog a clue to the direction it is expected to take when it cannot see the sheep at a National or International trial. If you intend to set the dog off to the left walk to the post with it at your left side. This is yet another clue for the dog, and he deserves all the help you can give him. It is quite true that your time does not begin until you have set the dog off, but this is no excuse for the many handlers who mess him about at their feet. This only tends to get him wound up with the result that he may cross his course or tighten at the far end of his outrun. As soon as you are at the post and the dog has seen the sheep, set him off quietly. The man letting sheep out should not be expected to hold them to the letting out post for an indefinite time. Personally, I would like to see the letting out post done away with altogether and the dog would then be judged from the point he picked the sheep up. Much controversy about the outrun and line would be settled in this way.

After setting off, the dog should make its way quickly but not hurriedly to the sheep. A dog which hurries will usually be tight at the top of the field. The shape of the outrun is a topic which can cause much controversy. The pear-shaped outrun is the best in my opinion; however, at the point where this meets the barometer-shaped outrun I begin to use my judging pencil. I do not condemn the square type and therefore do not deduct points from this providing that the square is of reasonable proportions. This is a question that the judge should decide upon and stick to throughout the day. An unreasonable square type outrun in my opinion occurs when the dog casts back behind the handler or continues at the same level for too great a distance. At the beginning of the day's judging I set a definite point on each side of the handler beyond which I consider the outrun to be unduly square and deserving of a deduction of points.

The argument for the square type is on its practical nature in hill gathering where one good swing may be more economical than several pear-shaped outruns and blow backs. The handler with National and International Trials in mind may prefer to play safe and err on the side of the too square outrun at the smaller trials. The argument for the pear-shaped outrun is that you set the dog off to gather a certain limited lot of sheep, and it should not and does not need to gather a whole area of ground to do it. Ideally the thing to aim at is to be able to communicate to the dog by the way you set it off, whether you want it to gather wide and square or more direct and pear-shaped. This is a thing that the dog will pick up gradually during its daily work.

The next part of the course which is intricately bound with the outrun is the lift. Its importance is often underestimated. This is the first time that the dog and sheep should come into contact and thus their first chance to form an impression of each other. This impression will affect the rest of the run. At a trial where the sheep are stiff it may pay the handler to lift them a little sharply, as they will then respect the dog for the rest of the run. If the sheep are light or flighty a little more time should be spent on the lift to allow the dog to feel them and take control of them. This, however, does not mean that the sheep should be allowed to stand and face the dog for a minute or more. The sheep should always be subjected to the dog's authority. The dog, having lifted the sheep, should take them in the straightest line possible to the fetch hurdle and then to the handler. During the fetch the handler's attention should be concentrated on the sheep's heads, as these will give warning of what their owners intend to do next. To be able to do this it is necessary for the handler to have implicit faith in the dog's response to his commands. By the time the expert handler is turning his sheep around him to begin the drive he will have them completely weighed up. The turn is another crucial point in the trial because this determines the direction of, and your control over, the drive. At the turn both dog and sheep are at your feet and you should take advantage of this fact to steady things down if they have been going a gear too high. Turn the steadied sheep with the dog in quiet but firm control and under your constant supervision. You will already have the position for the end of the turn and the beginning of the drive fixed firmly in your mind but a quick glance up at the drive hurdle will prove helpful. Before setting the dog in to drive, give the sheep a few seconds to get started, but take care not to let them get out of control of the dog. Most dogs flank a little tighter on the drive, so this extra few yards of distance between the dog and sheep will counteract the effect of the tighter flank.

The ideal speed at a trial is about as fast as it is possible for a dog to walk. This speed prevents sensible sheep from stopping to graze or running wildly in panic. The dog must always have control of the sheep and this speed will be found to be the ideal one for control. Even when the dog is stopped it should take the weight of the sheep and so remain in control of them. In theory the sheep should go through the dead centre of the hurdles for a perfect run. This may only be possible with very tractable sheep, which unfortunately are rarely met with south of the border and never north of it. The handler may then prefer to head his sheep towards the outside of the drive hurdle as the dog will flank quicker that way than to the inside. So if a quick flank is required to catch the hurdle let it be to the outside. A good tight unhurried turn at the hurdle sets a dog on the correct line for the crossdrive, and here again occasional glances at this obstacle help to keep the line in the handler's mind. The crossdrive is a long uncharted haul at some of the bigger trials. If possible it may prove advantageous to walk up the side of the course previously and plot the locations of thistles, tufts and patches of easily seen grasses. This will give you an additional clue to the position of your sheep at any one time. Having negotiated the hurdle the handler should bring the sheep to the pen mouth in as straight a line as possible. Stubborn sheep may be hurried a little here if time is running short; this may help them to realise the power of the dog before reaching the pen.

To say anything about the pen would be almost impossible. A million situations could and do arise each needing a different solution. The only advice therefore at this stage is not to panic the sheep into beginning circuits around the pen again and again. When this happens it is almost impossible to do any good with them. Pressure or patience may be the watchword, often a combination of a little of one alternating with a little of the other. If the sheep in the pen mouth begin to stare wildly about and their pupils begin to dilate, stop everything until peace reigns again. It is forbidden to touch the sheep at the pen but in desperate circumstances it is better to lose a few points by extreme measures rather than have the time whistle blown with the sheep still unboxed.

At one of the Dumfriesshire nursery trials in which I was competing, the sheep were very wild at the pen and no one was penning. After having quite a good run round the course with Jace, she brought the sheep almost to the pen mouth. I could see that they would become even wilder if I brought them any closer to me. The rope on the pen gate just seemed to be a yard too short. It was a cold drizzly day and the judge was sitting in his car a good distance away. I took a chance and let go of the rope so that I could take an extra step back, away from the pen. That one step was all the distance that was required. The sheep went straight into the pen and we won the trial. I have never asked the judge whether or not he noticed that I had let go of the rope. I suspect that he did, but still gave me sufficient penning points that put me above other good runs that failed to pen. Perhaps he gave me points for cheek!

After penning, never slam the gate as this only upsets the sheep for the shed and single. If, as is occasionally seen at trials, no one pens, then you have nothing to lose by what would normally be regarded as foolhardy. Patience and kindness not having paid off for anyone else it may not be amiss to try to dog the sheep into the pen. This, however, is a desperate cure.

Although it is nice to see a dog pen and shed, the handler must give it all the help that it requires. During everyday work at home, man and dog work always as a team. It would be ridiculous to give a dog no help at all when you are there with it at the pen. It would be equally ridiculous to do all the work yourself. The same principle applies to the job in hand on the trial field. "It is up to the dog outby so it is up to you to help it inby" was the advice once given to me by Jock Richardson. Time permitting, the opportunity for the shed or single invariably presents itself and must be taken promptly. Time not permitting, the opportunity must be made by the handler. At National or International trials there is neither time nor necessity for fancy work or fancy dogs. Do a determined workmanlike job. "Catch every hurdle and finish" must be the maxim uppermost in the handler's mind. Or as Tot Longton said to me, "You must have a sense of urgency at these big trials."

Another point which makes a great deal of difference at work or on the trial field is the distance between dog and sheep. Again for the theory behind this we can learn much from the work of Konrad Lorenz, in spite of the fact that he has probably never seen a dog working sheep. He explains how a physically superior animal like a tiger or a wolf will flee from an inferior one like a man providing that a certain and definite individual "fight distance" is not encroached upon. In other words the tiger will run as long as the man does not get too near it. If, however, this "flight distance" is shortened it becomes the "fight distance" and the tiger, or even an inferior animal, will then viciously attack its confronter. From this long realised observation the expression "fight like a cornered rat" evolved. When applied to sheep and dogs this theory can be seen to hold good. The sheep flee from the dog as long as it does not get any closer to them than their fight distance. If the dog gets too close they turn to face it and often cannot be moved even by the use of the dog's teeth. If, however, the dog is moved back beyond the fight distance into the flight distance, the same sheep will usually move away. The two mentioned distances vary to some extent between individual sheep. Members of the same flock however will have similar distances, and these can be and should be noted before the competitor goes to the post.

Anyone can win a trial, but it takes a man to lose. This was one of the first statements which impressed me when I began to run at trials. On the occasion of the English National trial at Dovedale, John Holliday was having an almost perfect run. Unfortunately, another dog ran on to the field and took charge of his sheep. A re-run was, of course, granted, to be judged from the point of the incident, but John could not get the same feeling again between his dog and the sheep, and thus failed to make the team. That night I spoke to John. He was not the angry man most of us would probably have been. He merely shrugged his shoulders and said, "These things happen". This is the kind of man who does the sport most good and is worthy of the respect of other handlers. Likewise after Jock Richardson's disaster in the Supreme Championship at Kilmartin he was man enough to be more concerned with looking forward to the next year's event rather than taking it out on everything from the officials to the kitchen sink. Therefore to the handler who has never won anything, I would say make the best of the situation and learn to lose in a fitting manner. Only then will you be worthy to hold your own with men of this calibre when your day comes.

A final piece of advice to the trialist concerns the method of getting the best out of his dog at these events. Don't practise too much at home. If you do, the dog may become indifferent and, when you go to the trial, he may think that you are still practising, and will not give you that extra bit you require of him. If, however, the maxim of "herd them and trial them, don't train them" is taken as a general rule, the dog will rise to the occasion at a trial, sensing that extra bit of urgency in the whistles. Obviously, if a dog had a bad habit at a trail you will have to cure it at home. This will entail some training and a lot of thought. For instance, a dog with a fault at the pen may need some penning practice at home, where both dog and handler are in a more congenial and unhurried mood. A pen will hardly require to be built for this as working the sheep into a tight corner of the field will usually be equally effective. In these highly competitive times trials are not training sessions, but perhaps there might be some laxity on this point at nursery trials.

One of the biggest thorns in the sides of trials competitors, apart from the judge, is the re-run. Generally speaking a man who is granted one has an enormous advantage over the rest of the field who walk to the post for the first time, and more often than not takes the money. The trouble is that granting a re-run because of bad sheep opens the judge to a barrage of questions or statements such as "his sheep were no worse than mine". It forces him to draw an impossibly fine line between one lot of sheep which warrant a re-run and another lot which are not quite bad enough. In theory once a competitor sets his dog off, he has accepted his chances for better or for worse. If any of his sheep prove to be unsound in mind or body during his fetch, he should ask the judge to examine them before he turns them on to the drive. Once his sheep are turned he has finally and definitely accepted them and has forfeited his right to ask for a re-run. This does not mean that the judge cannot grant a re-run after this point, only that the competitor must not ask for one.

So when should a judge grant a re-run? In very few cases, I think (except at nursery trials which should not be taken too seriously). Definitely in the case of sheep being unsound in body—i.e. blind or badly lame. Occasionally in the case of a sheep being of very unsound mind—i.e. climbing trees or totally shunning society. Hardly ever in the case of a competitor being given an unlucky break which puts him at an extreme disadvantage to his fellow handlers. By granting a re-run in this case, the judge effectively puts all other competitors under an extreme disadvantage. The judge cannot make or take a handler's luck—he can only point his run.

CHAPTER V

BREEDING

A DEEP knowledge of genetic theory is not essential for the breeding of the working dog. The most basic and elementary principles, however, may be useful for the breeder who wants to delve deeper into the subject. Certain characteristics or traits are passed on from parent to offspring, while other traits are not passed on because they are merely results of environment. For instance, if pups' tails are cut off for 100 or even 1000 generations, the pups of the 1000th generation will still have long tails. The docking was not a part of the dog's genetic make up, and therefore could not possibly be transmitted to the next generation. Likewise, black and white dogs will never breed pink dogs if they are dyed for one thousand generations, as the genetic make up will still remain unchanged.

Traits which can be passed on to the offspring are carried by the reproductive cells of the parents and combined in the pups in any one of numerous ways. Often traits from one parent completely overshadow traits from the other, in which case the dominant trait only is apparent in the pup. Less often a trait midway between those of its parents can be seen. A third alternative in the genetic lottery is that a trait which is present but hidden in the parents can become apparent in the pup. In a litter of pups various combinations may show up, and this explains why pups from the same litter range from good to indifferent or bad. In order to breed consistently good dogs it is therefore important not only that the visible traits are good but also the hidden ones as these will eventually come to the surface. The quality of the hidden traits can only be estimated by the study of whole families or by inbreeding.

The finished product, or broken dog, is roughly 50 per cent predetermined by its genetic make up and 50 per cent by its environment or breaking. The environment will depend on the skill of the handler. Thus, a dog with a perfect genetic make up will depend for the other 50 per cent on its handler. Likewise the perfect handler will depend for the other 50 per cent on his dog. So it follows that a 40 per cent handler with a 20 per cent dog will do better than a 10 per cent handler with a 40 per cent dog. Because of this it can be seen that in the selection of breeding stock only the genetic 50 per cent must be taken into account for the best chance of success.

It always gives me great pleasure and instruction to read success stories of professionals in every field of human achievement. Reading one such story several years ago on the occasion of the dispersal of the famous Vern herd of Hereford cattle, one particular statement struck me forcibly. The success of the herd was attributed to the talent of the owner in "knowing what he wanted and how to get it". From this it can be seen that the most fundamental point in breeding is to know what you want. This does not necessarily mean going to every international champion or popular stud dog generation after generation. These dogs may not be what you personally want, although presumably they are excellent. The breeder and handler should have the image of his perfect dog in his mind just as the judge should have his idea of the perfect run in his mind throughout the day of a trial. Even when the breeder sees the dog with most of the qualities that he wants, he must bear in mind two things. First, the dog may or may not have the ability to pass these qualities on to its offspring. Secondly, he must remember that the pups will be as much a product of the bitch herself as of the selected sire. It is also a distinct possibility that the near perfect dog will hardly ever breed its like. The dog with exaggerated strong points may in fact have a better chance of having them watered down to breed the near perfect dog. An hour spent among the stud books may prove to be an eye opener to the enthusiast who checks how many international champions have bred international champions, and it is, presumably, these dogs which get the most pups and have them distributed among the most competent handlers.

Nothing must take second place to temperament. According to a breeder and exhibitor of Alsatians, judges never look twice at a dog with a bad temperament. Obviously in the sheep dog world judges must not be influenced by a dog's temperament, but it is the breeder who should never look twice at this dog. These undesirable traits, although they may remain hidden for several generations, are still there and will re-appear on the surface at some time in the future. Nervousness, bad natures or genetic physical degeneracy must never be tolerated in the stud dog or breeding bitch. It is surprising how much can be overcome in the way of faults if the temperament is right. My own first dog, Shen, was short of power, and had too much eye, but because of her superb temperament she always gave of her very best. If I had tried to pen five bull elephants in a match box Shen would have worked to her full capacity until I called off the attempt. Thus I usually got away with her faults at trials and at work. Even when crossing a river with one hundred hoggs Shen would not be beaten even though it meant barking, tail throwing and "muttoning". A powerful dog with a bad temperament would not be able to give his master so much and would no doubt have abandoned the task as soon as the real pressure was on.

Neither must the breeder be fooled by the fancy dog. That is the dog with perfect turns and tremendous eye and style when things are going right. It is all very bonny. But a bonny dog is rarely any good when things are going wrong or when there is a real job of work to be done. Such a dog rarely causes a response in sheep that have their own ideas and thus is not in control of them. Look for the dog that is the master of every situation. He will be far more suitable to continue the breed than the fancy counterpart that is master of none. Many informed men place great importance on the tail in selecting a sire. It should be dead and without kinks. However, I will always use the dog that flags its tail merrily and turns the single sheep in preference to the dead tailed dog which is consistently beaten by the single sheep. Look at the dog's ability first and the finer points secondly.

Concerning inbreeding and line breeding, I once read the following statement: "If you breed closely related stock together with great success you attribute this to line breeding. If your results prove disastrous, you blame it on inbreeding". From this it can be seen that the breeding together of closely related stock may produce one of these two mentioned alternatives. The reason for this is quite easy to understand. The visible traits of closely related stock may be sound, but their hidden traits may or may not be. If the hidden traits are sound, line breeding which serves to concentrate the hidden and visible traits will produce good results. If, however, the hidden traits are unsound, when concentrated the results can only be disastrous.

There are two methods of determining the nature of the hidden traits. One is to line breed. The second is to have an intimate knowledge of the dog's ancestral family, including brothers and sisters of dogs which appear in the pedigree. A dog's hidden traits may occaionally occur in its ancestry. Even if the family has not been outstanding, as long as it is sound a fair chance of success may be expected. Very few people have the time and knowledge to study these ancestral families and assess them correctly. On the other hand, actual inbreeding is an undesirable practice for the amateur unless he is prepared for disaster at the end of the line. Inbreeding in man, fashionable in certain royal families at one time, usually leads to physical degeneracy and insanity. Because a dog is incapable of reasoning beyond simple cause and effect relationships, I doubt if insanity in the dog is possible. Dogs which are described as having a "screw loose" or as being "off their heads" are usually the result of bad handling or irresponsible rearing. Because of this it is the physically degenerate dog that is likely to be produced by inbreeding. This includes those with insufficient stamina, a defective conformation, bad temperament, plain weaklings and ill thriven dogs, traits which make themselves felt often enough without inbreeding.

The wise breeder will always know when to introduce the blood of a dog virtually unrelated to his own strain. Now that the breed and purity of the working collie have been firmly fixed, it is time to open up the stud book a little by making registration on merit easier. The fee should be reduced. This would encourage the man with an excellent unregistered dog or bitch to register it. Many such excellent dogs never win or even compete at a trial, and so I would prefer to see an inspection by a knowledgeable official replace the present placings rule. This influx of new blood could only help the breed. In these days, because a few notable sires are used to an extent never before known, it is difficult to find a registered outcross. Let us take care not to dry up the genetic pool.

As a slight divergence on registration I would mention the Haflinger Horse Society, which inspects every single Haflinger in Austria when it reaches the age of three. If it falls short of the high standard set by the Society it is not accepted for registration. Thus a registered Haflinger really means something. This is far more than can be said for the registered Border Collie. I cannot see this ever happening in the Border Collies because of the tremendous amount of work and expense involved. For the present I would be satisfied with the opening up of the stud book to the many excellent everyday dogs.

After the selection and use of the stud dog, the pups will be born roughly 63 days later. They should be inspected frequently as a pup may easily stray from its brothers and sisters and be left in the cold. If a sack is used for bedding, a pup may be caught and lost in a loose fold. The pups usually open their eyes when they are ten days old. At this time the breeder should encourage them to lap milk (at blood heat) by pushing their noses into it. Holding them under for long periods is not advisable. Some pups seem to get the idea within a day or two while others take a week or more. However, by the time they are one month old they should all be taking a little milk and baby food or other suitable feed. This should be given at least three times a day and an odd rabbit may be thrown to them now and again. It is important to worm them at three weeks old as the worm burden will already have started to build up by this time. Cod liver oil, good food, exercise, cleanliness and warmth are among the most important requisites for the litter of pups. By now the bitch will be spending more time away from them. She should still not be worked hard, or for prolonged periods or the milk may heat and upset the pups. She will require an increase in her feeding and should be given as much as she will eat. The best way to starve the pups is to starve the bitch. If the pups are healthy they should be seen to be growing and have a good appetite and playful manner. They can be weaned completely between six and seven weeks, and only after this time should they be sent to their new homes. It is up to the breeder to see that the pups have been handled as much as possible from their birth until they leave his kennels. After that it is up to the new owners to see that their development and education continue unchecked.

CHAPTER VI

WILLIAM CAIG (1881-1968)

IF the fireside chairs in the herd's cottage at Crookedstane, Elvanfoot knew nothing about dogs and handlers it was their own fault. For their occupiers spent many an hour discussing the subject. Long after the clock had shown the midnight hour Willie Hainey and myself chewed over doggy problems and experiences. On these occasions the name of William Caig constantly came to Willie's lips in his endeavours to keep me on the straight and narrow.

"As a dog handler I think William Caig had no equal," said Willie. "There was a tremendous understanding between him and his dogs. He could see and develop small things into greatness. I remember a bitch, Nan — I don't think she ever ran at a trial — who had the habit of investigating anything unusual. By the time she was two years old this had been developed to the pitch where she could be relied on to 'look' a bad drowning place on the hill. If Nan passed the place you could be sure that no sheep were in trouble there. All his dogs seemed to use the minimum amount of force needed for the job in hand. Like the man handling them they were always master of the situation."

The war, however, came at a crucial time in William Caig's career. "I often wonder what heights he might have reached had it not been for this. About that time he had a dog called Rover, sired by Lord Mostyn's Coon and out of his own Betty. I thought that Rover was the greatest dog I had ever seen. I remember him mainly for his ability to find sheep in the snow and his ability to 'ken' them. When driving a single beast, if he let her mix amongst a score of sheep or more, Rover would 'ken' her and bring her out again. He was one of the best dogs I ever knew for hill or trial work."

It was because of Willie's great respect for the late William Caig that he put me in touch with Mrs. S. Ferguson, his daughter, who kindly loaned me some of her father's notes. Neatly and meticulously written at the beginning of his record book is the reference to the Castle Douglas Trial — the first in Galloway. "In the first week of April 1900 a trial was held in conjunction with the Cattle Show at which I was present as a spectator. There was an exhibition given of two dogs working by Joseph Moses, Brogntyn, Wales, with his two small grey coloured dogs. All his directions were given by whistles which they obeyed with remarkable intelligence. I had never seen anything like it, and it left a lasting impression."

48

Herding in the saddle is becoming increasingly popular where vast tracts of ground have to be covered. This view was taken at the head of Weststonedale, an off-shoot of Swaledale.

(Tom Parker)

Michael Perrins with his International Shepherds' Champion, Kyle, drives his flock away after inspection.

(K. & J. Jelley)

The moment of tension as Jim Cropper pens his sheep with his illustrious Fleet at the Chester International Championship. Fleet made his debut in the Pennine Nursery Trials and went on to be "capped" for England many times.

(Farmers Guardian)

"Waiting to compete". A study taken at the Yorkshire Open Trial in 1977

A judges' eye view as Tim Longton competes with Roy at Buttermere
for the 1975 Television Sheepdog Trophy.

(Lance Alderson)

Two dogs patiently wait their turn at the Mallerstang sheepdog trials.

(Bertram Unne)

Llyr Evans with the renowned Bosworth Coon, Supreme International Champion at Towyn in 1968 and runner-up at Chester the following year.

(Nicholas Meyjes)

David Carlton and Tony at home at Chipping, Lancashire. Tony won the English Shepherds' Aggregate Trophy at the Lockerbie Internationals in 1976, and also the English heat for the 1977 Television Sheepdog Trophy at Austwick, Yorkshire.

(W. Wilkinson)

A familiar figure at the Pennine trials, Johnny "Whistler" Wilkinson with one of his dogs.

David McTier with Ben, Shepherds' Champion at the Newcastle Internationals in 1972. Ben was also the Scottish National Champion in the same year.

(Scottish Farmer)

Jock Richardson with the legendary Wiston Cap (centre) and his two sons, Sweep (left) and Mirk — all champions in their own right.
(Matt Mundell)

Again in 1906 Mr. Caig refers to another trial held at Castle Douglas with a large entry of 31 dogs, 14 of which were from Wales and England. However, his record of the innovation of Gatehouse Trial in 1905 is the most comprehensive. "Gatehouse Trial started on New Year's Day 1905. Prior to that a dog show was held in the Town Hall with a class for shepherds' dogs. I remember showing my dog in 1904 and got a prize too, but was so sorry for him drawn up by the neck to a ring in the floor all day, that I said never again. A Gatehouse gentleman of that date, Mr. Grimshaw, had similar thoughts for he said, "Why! this is no place for a sheepdog. Give him a few sheep out in a field and let's see what he can do with them, and I'll give you a cup for the first prize." He was taken at his word and the result was a trial in the Garries Park on New Year's Day 1905. The weather was favourable and a large crowd of spectators turned out to see it. The first prize was won by James Halliday, Laghead, with a bare black and tan dog, Clyde.

"In 1907 Ben Murray came down from Minnigryle and won with Tam. This was a great show, the best work we had seen at the Gatehouse. The trial was still confined to Kirkcudbrightshire, and the question arose was Minnigryle in the County. The boundary burn comes down through the middle of the farm. The house was in Dumfriesshire, as also was the hirsel Ben herded. This problem was solved by a motion being put forward that the trial be open to all comers and let the best dog win. Ben had entered off Pointfoot, Dalry, which was the hirsel in Kirkcudbrightshire, but it was herded all that time by the single herd. Ben was a master handler of a dog. No running about gesticulating or shouting. Just wee peeps of whistles that were instantly responded to, and he never stirred off the spot himself. I remember going home and saying to my wife I envy no man his silver or his gold but I wish I had a dog and could work it like Ben Murray.

"Again in 1908 Ben Murray won the trial with a ten month old beardie and was second with Tam, last year's winner. Ben was very proud, as well he might be, of winning with his 10 month old pup. He was later sold for £11 to Joseph Moses who called him Jock and for some years cleaned up much prize money in England and Wales. Eleven pounds was the most we had ever heard paid for a dog."

Perhaps the most amusing story in these early records is that concerning the 1922 event which was judged by Jos Murray of Corsebank, Sanquhar. "When 'Corsebank' started judging first he had a habit of standing close behind the competitor and working him whilst he worked his dog. For instance, once at Dalry in Waterside Holm, George Caig had a bitch Jed, running out fine and wide (so he thought). Suddenly 'Corsebank' at his back shouts, 'Hut, toot, toot! Far too wide. Stop your dog and pull her in.' Well, there was the judge speaking. He whistled. Jed, obedient, stopped. He cried her in and she came with a beautiful sweep through between him and the sheep and lifted off the wrong side, I dare not write all that was said.

"That year the trial was won by Alex Millar with Roy beating Jame McInlay's Hawker and William Wallace's Loos (1 year). However, 'Corsebank' must have made quite a good job of judging that year because he was invited to judge again the next year (1923). On this occasion Sandy Millar stayed with us at Kilmafadzean the night of New Luce trial. Next day was Gatehouse and 'Corsebank' the judge. At breakfast Sandy says, 'Gor' man, I've a guid min' to tell yon buddy, if he's ocht to say to me to say it afore I start and not be roarin' in ma lug when I'm workin' ma dug.' That year he (Corsebank) was proposed as a judge for the Nationals. This 'hobby' of his was mentioned and straight away a rule was made. If a judge has anything to say to a competitor, he must do so through the course director. 'Corsebank' took the hint and was a good judge ever after."

Another point of interest recorded by Mr. Caig concerns his brother George's dog, Tyne. Tyne was sixth in the Gatehouse open trial and also won Bargrennan trial in 1921 at 20 months old. "It was a grand wee dog out of Tom Ferguson's bitch by Sweep. At six months old he was the best I had seen. His masterpiece was 'coupies.'* he could wind them and lift them too. Once out on Glenap on a misty day he put his nose to the wind, which was in the west, and started off. George knew his attitude and followed up over the top of Bengray (over the marsh dyke) and down on to the flat ground on high Creoch. There she (the coupie) was lying kicking her heels in the mist, two miles from the spot where he first winded her."

Not only is this a remarkable feat of canine "intelligence" but more so it is a glimpse of the calibre of "herds of yesteryear." How many men of today would have the understanding and character to follow their dog two miles over the boundary wall on to a neighbour's land to lift a coupie?

William Caig, as well as being a poet, humorist, historian and competent dog handler, was also a philosopher. He obviously gave the same deep thought to every problem and would then announce his views and verdicts without fear or favour. The following untitled extract from his notebook shows the soundness of his well thought out views and also gives a glimpse of some of this outstanding man's many facets: "There is no good flock without a good shepherd behind it and no good shepherd without a good sheep dog behind him. One half of the shepherd's equipment is to be a good kener and to ken his sheep. The other half is to have a good sheepdog to help him. Recently I saw a query in the *Scottish Farmer* asking at what age to start training a sheepdog; the answer given was ten months old. I do not agree. At Gatehouse trial in 1908 the first prize in the open class was won, and worthily won, by Ben Murray, Minnigryle, with a puppy

*'Coupie' is a Scottish term for a sheep which has rolled onto her back and is unable to get up without assistance.

exactly ten months old. Later on, in the hands of Joseph Moses, it was a leading dog in England and Wales. His early start did him no harm. Again in 1919 at the same trial the second prize in the open class was awarded to another 10 month old pup of which I was the proud owner. The pup is born into the shepherd's household, and as soon as he can run about he learns to answer his name. He learns to lie down when told, to lead on a string and to follow at heel:

> *He romps aboot among the bairns,*
> *And even there he sometimes learns;*
> *While mixin' in their gleeful' game,*
> *And as they scamper o'er the mead,*
> *They teach him on the string to lead.*

"Whenever he shows an inclination to work, let him work — keep a watchful eye on him, do not let him chase stragglers, steady a few sheep at hand with an old dog and let the pup run about them. That is good enough for some time. Give him a little encouragement when he does well. Stop him when he is going wrong and he will grow into it by degrees just as the willow that grows by the waterside grows into a tree. Many a time a bundle of excited energy has trotted up to my feet with a yearning steady gaze. Looking down at the pair of sparkling eyes I have there seen something that said as plain as words, 'I'm ready and willing and anxious to help, to serve, to love you, if only you show me how.' The word 'training' applied to a puppy jars upon my ears. It implies something that you put into it and perhaps rub it well in with a cleckie — all wrong of course. It's all there already, bred in that wee brainbox waiting to be drawn out and developed."

CHAPTER VII

VIEWPOINT

EVERY handler has his own particular style which he builds up partly by watching other successful handlers and partly by a system of trial and error. The methods and opinions of most successful handlers in the sheepdog world are always interesting and informative in their own right. When set down next to each other they prove doubly interesting in the comparison. It is for this reason that I have interviewed and recorded my conversations with some of these men.

Holding the record of being first and second in the Supreme Championship at Stirling in 1967 with his home bred mother and daughter is Mr. T. T. McKnight. To this remarkable achievement he also added the International Brace Championship, the Scottish Driving Championship and first and third placings in the qualifying trials with the same dogs, Gael and Dot, in that year. Farming near Canonbie, Thomson McKnight milks 25 cows and lambs 120 ewes. Because of the limited amount of work available for the dogs he likes them to start as naturally as possible. He does not like the young dog to be a bad gripper or have any other serious faults, but is willing to tolerate a grip in the young dog if he likes everything else about it.

"In my own particular circumstances a young dog must behave itself. Although I think a rough young dog could easily improve if a lot of work is available for it. The colour is quite important too. I like a sensibly marked black and white dog or a black, white and tan dog, as these seem to have a better effect on the sheep than the all black or all white dog. It should also be well put together and of a fair size so that the sheep will respect it." Thomson does not like the young dog to be excessively clappy but also adds, "The young dog which is one hundred per cent upstanding as a pup strangely enough seems to develop into a lazy dog at middle age and rarely lasts into old age."

He likes a stylish dog, although he says, "This has nothing to do with its capabilities. Most people's opinions of what they want to see in a dog are influenced by their own first successful dog. Mine was stylish and fairly nippy. I was also influenced quite considerably by J. M. Wilson's Nap, and he was a fast stylish dog. A dog must be purposeful and a stylish dog usually looks it. It certainly must not stick but I do not like to see a dog come in amongst sheep off hand unless it has been asked to do so by its handler. This is only permissible when sheep have provoked the dog unduly. At the pen the dog is better on its feet if the sheep are facing it, but if they are looking away from the dog it is not as important.'

What, during his career of watching and competing at trials, stands out in Thomson's mind as being particularly memorable? "Worthington's Juno had a tremendous method when she was working her sheep, she controlled them with determination and knowledge. Jock Richardson's outruns at Cardiff with Wiston Cap were exceptional and could not be forgotten by anyone who saw them. In 1958, even though it was early in my career and I was perhaps more impressionable, I still have a vivid picture of John Evans winning the Supreme Championship with Tweed. He was a complete dog, good outruns, plenty of power and extremely classy. One particular sheep really tested him in the shedding ring. Tweed wore it to perfection, never flinching and never doing anything rash. When he put his head down and came on to the sheep, they just had to come. There was no doubt about the winner when Tweed had finished. I liked to see John Evans compete. He was a most polished handler, no rough edges, a potential winner every time he walked to the post."

I asked Thomson about Gael, his Stirling winner in 1967. She was a smooth-coated bitch of great determination and character. "Her mother Dot died when she was only four years old. At that time Gael was booked to go to New Zealand but because of Dot's death she stayed with me. I still remember the first time she saw sheep, it was the first of October when the wintering hoggs came to the farm. She was six months old, but as there were no other sheep on the farm at that time, she had not previously had the chance to see any. She started to work immediately. She was a bit fast at first but was always a great wearer and very stylish. By the time she was two years old I began to trial with her, and at her third trial (which was Drymen) she won a third place. Unfortunately, I did not start to keep records until 1964, but from then onwards she won £750. I think she must have topped the £1,000 all told. No bitch has ever both run as well and bred as well as Gael. She was a great work bitch. The night before the Internationals I took her up the fields to give her a practice. Two cows had just calved and we had to set off home with them. That turned out to be Gael's last run before the Internationals because by the time we got home it was dark. Even so I was still very confident at Stirling and more so on the last day because Gael was always consistent at the big job. She was so easily corrected that it helped my confidence greatly."

Thomson was very vociferous in the praise of the International championship course and especially of Mr. J. Reid, who designed it. "The man was a genius, he had no practical experience to speak of, yet he produced this course which has stood the test of time. It has remained virtually unchanged since the beginning and cannot be improved on with the facilities available. It is a great and practical test of the working dog."

My next journey through Tweedsmuir took me past the many one time hill farms that are now ruthlessly planted with trees. It was strangely reminiscent of a graveyard, each tree being the headstone for a ewe that had formerly grazed these slopes. Then, emerging once again into living country, I came to the Peebles road and followed it until the sign-post for Manor pointed the way over the river Tweed. Following this road for a short distance eventually brought me within sight of the small picturesque cottage of Milton Manor where Mr. David McTier lives. Here he herds 500 Blackface ewes and 100 hoggs on 1,000 acres of hill ground. David, the 1970 International Champion with Bill III, is no stranger to the International field. The supreme honour had previously eluded him by only 1½ points in 1964 with Mirk. On that occasion he carried off the second place in the Supreme Championship, but won the Shepherd's Championship and the Driving Championship.

"The first thing I look for in a young dog," said David, "is honesty. In fact, that is the first thing I look for in any animal or any man. It is something in the way they look at you. If it is there it can be seen immediately. An honest dog will never let you down when you are in difficulties. I also like to see a well laid on tail that comes down nice and tight to the hocks and then bends away without curling up. I do not want to see any movement in his tail. A young dog with a bad tail would have to be really outstanding before I would bother with it at all. It should show natural ability from the start and cast off when it reaches sheep. I would not like to see it just batter on; in fact, I prefer the young dog not to be too bold or too confident at this stage. Neither should he be too strong in the eye. His eye should never stop him coming forward, but be sufficient to hold his concentration on sheep and keep his carriage right. I do not like a dog to be clappy when it is not being commanded. It does not have to be too stylish as long as it is easy moving and fluid. A dog should be happy when he gets with his sheep, he should not have to be severely controlled or strongly encouraged. A steady dog has the confidence and knowledge that sheep will move for him. The dog that has to rush at sheep does so because of a certain deficiency within himself. The dog's looks do not make any difference if he is good enough, but I do not think a white dog would be worth bothering with for trials, as they certainly tend to draw sheep on to themselves. However, a dog's stamina and ability to last the years is very important, and a thing which we should perhaps take more notice of in breeding dogs. I like to see a dog like Tot Longton's Rob that still proved itself capable even though well advanced in years."

Did any dog stand out in David's mind as being particularly notable? "It is hard to say, but I remember being very impressed by Buist's Roy at the Inverness National in 1965. He was a good flanker, a good stopper and a nice dog to manage. He had an excellent method and control over his sheep. In fact, he was everything you could wish for."

What factors had influenced David's own style of running and his opinions? "I often used to go up to Davy Murray's at Glenbield and watch him working his dogs. He was a great man, a gentleman of the sheepdog world. I never once heard him run down any man or dog. He always impressed me with his own coolness and the fact that he never got excited about doing any job. The type of dog he ran was powerful and steady, and that was the kind I wanted to run." David stressed that this type of dog was the easiest to do your work with and would usually have a natural follow. They could also be trusted to do a lot of work on their own without command. "I remember taking Mirk to Davy Murray's. I told him that a lot of people were saying he was too good too soon and would deteriorate. Davy said, 'A right one will never go wrong'."

I asked David about his own two successful dogs, Bill III and Mirk. "I got Bill as a service pup and began to take him to the hill when he was six months old. For two months he showed no interest whatever till one day when two hoggs jumped up right out from in front of us. Bill chased them a little and then returned. We walked on and the next lot of sheep we came across Bill gathered. He developed into a good everyday type of dog with a great follow although he was often a bit hard to manage in the beginning. I was confident with him on the final day because he preferred the big stuff."
I spoke to David about the pen at the end of his championship course where the sheep were wild and determined not to go in. "It was hair-raising, but Bill was tremendously clever at countering the fast moves of wild sheep, and I knew I would have to leave it up to him."

Even though it was Bill that won the Supreme title for David, he seemed to have a soft spot for Mirk. "Mirk had that much common sense he could just learn a thing right away. He began to run at six months old and competed in his first trial at 1 year 3 months. He died eleven years to the day from his first trial. In those days I herded 32 score and Mirk was the only dog I had. It did not matter what went wrong, Mirk could always cool a situation and pull you out of it. He would handle any kind of sheep whether they were wild or stiff, and the International driving championship was just up his street. The more sheep he had the better he went, and he somehow relayed his confidence to me. When he was bringing his second lot of sheep at the Drymen International, he saw the first lot and put them together without any command from me. It was just his common sense and knowledge. Never once in ten competitive seasons did he let me down, he was so honest."

What were David's views about trials and the sport in general? "I do not like a trial course to be like a circus as this encourages circus dogs, and that is one thing I do not like. It should be kept as near the practical job as possible. I think that there is no real need for a fetch hurdle, the dog should know that he should bring sheep directly to his handler. Also some of the pens you see at trials are hardly the kind you would build at home if you wanted to box sheep in on

63

the hill for some reason. But on the whole it is a great sport; it is unique in the fact that it is all up to you and the dog. There is no one to cover up for you as in some of the team games like football. Most of all you must enjoy the competitive spirit, but you must also be able to accept a beating in the same way as you accept the top placing."

It was a familiar road up through Biggar and Newbiggin to Dunsyre. Here at Weston, Jock Richardson herds 28 score of Cheviots in parks. He had previously had a spell herding the hill at Menzion, which is now just another area of forest, in Tweedsmuir. Before that he was the park herd at Lyne from where he won the Supreme Championship in 1965 with the legendary Wiston Cap, and was the Shepherd's Champion in 1966. Jock has always been in country service. At one time he led a Clydesdale stallion round in a certain district to serve the local working mares. His introduction into the sheepdog world, however, was when he worked as a dairyman and used a dog to bring in the cattle. His interest grew and he was given a registered bitch by Bob Frame. He used to take this bitch up to Will Sykes, the shepherd at Hazelside, who often broke dogs for farmers and also trialled locally. It is Will Sykes that Jock credits with putting him on the right lines and giving him the basic ideas of what is needed in a dog. In those days the maggot was a considerable problem and sheep had to be brought right to the shepherd and caught in the open field. For this reason Will Sykes would never have a dog that turned tail. He wanted a good outrun and a dog on its feet.

What does Jock like to see in a young dog? "Natural potential, a nice shape as early as possible and gradually improving. A pup that goes out and shows nice eye and is on his feet is good to work with. It is very important that he has a kindly nature and is friendly. All young dogs have some faults but I look for the good bits about him. A dog should be like a dog and a bitch like a bitch. It is the same with everything; the male should be bigger and stronger than the female. I do not like a red dog or a white one for trailing as they cause the sheep to look round to see what is behind them. At lambing time, lambs tend to run to a white dog. They may, however, be excellent dogs at home on sheep that are used to them."

Jock does not particularly like a light eye as this could be a sign of hardness, and conversely a dark eye could be a sign of softness. "I like to see a 'dead' tail," says Jock, "whatever the dog is doing. A tail that flags about indicates uncertainty and a lack of confidence."

We then spoke about the broken dog. "It must run out well and cover its sheep, overlapping rather than stopping short. I like to see a natural bit when the dog is bringing the sheep to the handler. He should be upstanding and easy flanking. I like the dog to have eye and style; in fact I would not keep a plain dog. But when the eye causes the dog to stare at sheep it is no good because he will not flank or do what you ask him. Neither does the plain dog have the balance needed, so he does not find the steadying point."

64

Had any particular dogs impressed Jock during his career? "Hugh's Jaff. I saw him at Ayr and thought he was the greatest thing I had ever seen. He was in a class of his own. What power! He was in the driving championship that day and the way he could put sheep together and push them on was tremendous. Hislop's Sweep was the first dog I saw to have a full pointed run. He was very impressive too. As for precision work, J. M. Wilson's Nap would take some beating. He had tremendous movement and was really strong in his good points."

I asked Jock about his own dog, Wiston Cap, the Cardiff winner in 1965. Jock had worked on the Cap (3036) line until he eventually bred a half white-faced dog — old Cap. He was a very useful, sound dog and always ran well until his tragic death at the sheep pens when he was only six years old. He was mated to a mild bitch that had some nice natural bits about her. Jock had seen her wearing a single sheep on the hill and, being impressed by this, he took one of her pups when she came to old Cap. "This pup was Wiston Cap. He worked at three months old, and what a nature he had. Even as a pup he used to follow me into the house at dinner time and sit beside the chair. He never bothered about anything else round him and was afraid of nothing. He started naturally, wore sheep on his feet and showed nice eye and balance. Everything seemed easy to him. If I showed a thing to him once he had it right. He never disagreed with anything I tried to teach him and was always consistent. He was a tremendous herding dog, I could lay him on to sheep about the pens and take him to a trial the next day."

How did Jock feel on the final day at the Cardiff International? "Nervous. I bought four bottles of ginger beer and drank the lot. It was the first time I had ever qualified and never thought about winning or being confident. I just wanted to go out there and run to the best of my ability. I did not want to let Cap down, because he had been such a great dog for me in everyday work. In fact, I am still nervous when running my dogs, but their natures are right. We are pals, and because of this bond between us they help me. It is a kind of telepathy developed by being together in everyday work."

What about Sweep and Mirk, his two sons of Wiston Cap that have both brought Jock International honours? "I have the same feeling for them as I have for Cap. They are two different types of dog; Mirk is a natural trial dog and Sweep is an outstanding hill dog because of his tremendous distance and power."

Jock likes to see a good dog, regardless of blood lines, and thinks that most dogs could win a trial given the right sheep. "I think we breed more good dogs now than we did ten or fifteen years ago; they have a better line and are easier commanded although they are not as hard as they used to be. We need an easily commanded dog because on a trial field the obstacles are there to be negotiated. It also has a practical aspect as well; you may have to bring sheep over a shallow part of a stream on a distant hillside. Eventually, however, we may have to come back to the more powerful type of dog, now that deildrin has been taken out of the dips and the maggot may become a menace again. We should go in for a type of dog that incorporates trialling ability with everyday work."

Jock is attracted to the sport of trialling because being a herd he works with dogs every day. "I like to see other dogs and let people see mine in the competitive atmosphere. We must always run dogs for the love of it and not for the financial side. Those who see only the prize money never see any good points in a dog but only the bad ones. No dog is perfect, but look for the things that you like about it."

Branching off the road that winds through the Trough of Bowland just a short way from Quernmore, the traveller, by following the Rooten Brook sign, eventually climbs into the yard of Tim Longton's farm. It was here, sitting in the hot midday sun, that I spoke to Tim about his views and experiences in the sheepdog world. He, his brother Tot and their cousins, the Huddlestons, have served England well on the International field where in 1966 Tim carried off the coveted Supreme trophy. Tim and his son farm 723 acres, most of which is high hill ground. The stock consists of approximately 140 cattle and a flock of 450 Dalesbred sheep producing pure and crossed lambs.

"Temperament is the first thing I look at; it is most important that this is right. The size is quite important too, I do not like a very big dog, as it tends to be too clumsy. Because of this it may not be a good work dog. I would rather have a smaller dog, as it will often do much more work." Tim cited his own little Nell, who was the Shepherds' Champion in 1951. "She was only a small bitch but she never seemed to tire."

Tim thought very highly of Nell, and told me about one of her more memorable escapades. She was once bringing sheep home from the fell together with several other men and dogs. Two lambs were giving Nell a lot of trouble. As she worked one, the other moved further away from the flock. She was working at a distance from Tim and entirely under her own initiative when she eventually left one lamb and worked the other right into the centre of the flock. Returning for the first lamb, she found that it had made its way through the fence and mixed with another large flock of sheep. "When we got to the bottom of the fell," said Tim, "there was Nell with the lamb waiting at the gate. She had sorted it out all alone and without a single command."

The dog's tail caused Tim to comment, "I do not like it to curl, especially if the curl is over to the side. A dog should not show too much eye. In fact, I would rather it started a little on the rough side with plenty of 'get-at-em'. It should just have enough eye to keep its head and tail down and to keep the dog itself in order." Tim was very definite when he said, "I must like a dog or I just will not bother with it." When evaluating a broken dog, Tim says, "It must be a good work dog first of all, with good gathers. It must mean everything and transmit this to the sheep by its method of working. I would rather see a dog working on the hill if I was thinking of using it as a stud dog. I like to see a dog relaxed when it is at work."

What factors had influenced Tim's method of handling and his opinions? "Most of it has been handed down from my father, but I watch everybody and try to use the good things that I see them do and avoid the bad. I remember seeing W. J. Evans at a trial. The crossbred Lonks were almost impossible to pen and everybody was pressing them hard to try and get them in. He just stood back and flicked his hands at them and they walked right in. He also made the best shed I have ever seen, with Roy at the Yorkshire Trials."

I asked Tim about Ken, his own Supreme Winner. "I got him from Norman Woods when he was above a year old and I liked the way he handled sheep in a workman-like manner. He was the master of every situation; I never put him in a situation that he failed to get out of. When it came to penning sheep Ken was wonderful. At the Leicester Nationals, in the doubles class, my sheep were extremely difficult at the pen but he kept pressing and giving until he got them. He was as good on cattle as he was on sheep, in fact I think a kick from a cow was the cause of the tumour from which he died. He never reserved himself on cows. I once saw him almost knocked unconscious by a kick but still going forward. Ken was running so well at the time of the Internationals that I felt it would be easy. He lifted his sheep just hard enough but that let them know that they had to go for him."

About trialling in general Tim said, "We must keep it in perspective. Although we want to win, the money should not be everything. I also think that it would be possible to get a bigger following for the sport through better organisation perhaps. The public must know what is going on, or they will lose interest."

To find a man not personally involved in competitive handling yet sufficiently knowledgeable and informed on international running might have been a formidable task. Fortunately, I knew Harold Walker of Waddington, a small Lancashire village near Clitheroe. Harold had watched the Supreme Championships intently since 1949 and had only missed two of them up to 1973. I asked him to reach back in time for the dogs that were outstanding in his opinion as a spectator. "John Holliday's Moss at the Loughborough Championships had controlled and determined power, and backed the big heavy sheep right into the pen. Jackie McDonald's Mirk was a very natural type of dog that was handled without fuss and with minimum command. Things looked easy for him, especially in the shedding ring where the sheep just walked off quietly and steadily. In fact, I think he won the prize for minimum command that year."

Harold clearly remembered the brace run by W. Work with his two dogs. He had penned the first lot of sheep with Ken and then went to pen the second lot. "Ken sneaked a few yards from the pen mouth and the sheep came out. Without moving away from the second pen Mr. Work pushed the sheep back into the first pen with Ken. It was a remarkable feat." He was also impressed by Wiston Cap, the 1965 Cardiff winner. "Jock had great command over him. His outfield work was exceptional. He knew he was going to do a job and did it properly. He was an easy worker and never flogged himself unnecessarily. David Murray was another exceptional handler who impressed me. He always worked his dogs very quietly. I remember Vic on his outrun jumping into the outlet pen. Davy just whistled quietly and Vic jumped out at the other side and carried on as though nothing had happened, picking up his allotted sheep. When it comes to running two dogs Ivor Hadfield takes some beating; he runs them quietly and there is always real co-operation between the dogs. He has given some tremendous demonstrations, especially with Mick and Roy. I always liked to see J. M. Wilson competing. He was a very canny handler and the master of every situation. When he had penned his five sheep with Bill, the 1955 winner, he let them out of the pen and sent Bill for the other 15 sheep. After setting him off, 'J.M.' turned his back and walked away. Bill brought the lot without any further command."

Other dogs which stand out in Harold's mind were Hugh's Jaff and Longton's Nell. "Jaff was a great driving dog who had plenty of sense. He set his pace to suit the sheep and had absolute control over them. A real practical dog with strength and power. Nell, too, was a practical dog that you could take to work with every confidence. A type of dog that I admire for sheer working ability was Bob Fraser's, they could really get the work done having the outruns and pressure needed."

What kind of things did Harold look for as he sat in the stand assessing dogs and runs? "I like to see real co-operation between man and dog. The dog must respond to every command, especially outfield, and the handler should be one jump ahead of the sheep in his handling. I prefer the free moving dog with moderate speed, he must be interested in his work and have the power to do it. Quiet handling is another thing I like to see, the quieter the better. It is merely a question of stockmanship. Any animal responds better if it is handled quietly. The noisy competitor cannot electrify his dog in a desperate situation if he is shouting and bawling all the time." Harold concluded by saying, "All dogs have some weakness but the good all-rounder is the dog for me."

To complete the spectrum of sheepdog enthusiasts the final viewpoint is expressed by Matt Mundell. He is the editor of the popular *Scottish Sheepdog Handler* and trials reporter for the *Scottish Farmer*. One evening before setting off for the south of England in his capacity as journalist, Matt penned the rest of these lines at my request.

"Whether there will be many herds and hill men left in the future to attend herds' fairs and the like I do not know. Here in Galloway and also in Tweedsmuir they are a vanishing people. As you know yourself, men and dogs are leaving the hills every week, and forestry ploughs are coming in. When a man leaves a hill, in a big number of cases he leaves an empty cottage. Just the other week I was up a glen with more than twenty cottages where once herds and their families lived. These folk will never return. Nor, unless something miraculous happens, will their families come back, as more and more get caught up in the whirl and disillusionment of the '70s and a city type of life. Here in Galloway, where drift from rural areas is worse than in the more publicised Highlands, many more schools will be closing, many more homesteads will become empty. Mobile shops pack up; postmen might call on the few folk that are left in the glen twice a week in future. My main argument against trees is that I feel if some of our younger farmers and shepherds could get the same encouragement as some of the private forestry groups they could make them far more viable and bring hope where now there is only blackness closing in over us. So that is why I enjoy and welcome functions such as herds' suppers, the increasing number of sheepdog dinners and sheepdog trials in particular. These folk are taking more responsibility for meeting the challenge of keeping alive our rural heritage. Long may the organisers of trials and dinner/functions carry on, for we badly need folk and organisations to keep up the momentum of rural life.

"I sometimes wonder after looking back through old newspaper clippings, letters, books, etc., if we have characters of the calibre of yesterday. I would doubt it. But I would like to think that from dinners, suppers and sheepdog trials we can strive to help and encourage more folk, especially younger herds and farmers, to come and try their skill and improve it. I have no doubt that this will help to instil character and pride in their duties. Some conservationists tell us the urban folk will be flocking in future years into the countryside to enjoy walking through the forests. I cannot see anyone flocking to the many thousands of acres in this direction to wade mile after mile through Sitka spruce and see decayed cottages, broken buchts, tumbledown dykes and the like. I am certain they would rather drive up our glens where they could see lambs, sheep on the hills, dogs gathering and tidy farm homesteads and herds' cottages.

"The collie can still be improved in the hands of good shepherds and farmers, through breeding. But never turn it into a machine. We can never do without their inborn intelligence and initiative. Sometimes it might not be needed so much on the 'table tennis' trial field but it is essential when far out on the hill. Maybe in fact it is some of our Saturday trials courses that help to turn the collies into machines. I wish one or two organisers of trials would be a bit more adventurous and for once try something different — lay out the course differently or find a new course on a big natural hill and work on natural objects (burns, gullies, etc.) rather than gates. We want dogs that can use their own heads as well as listen to commands.

"The only trouble with trials is that they are too far from home. Many a time I am up at 3 a.m. to traipse north and arrive back after midnight. On a Sunday morning once, when scowling bleary eyed over the porridge, our youngster came up and said, 'Daddy, are you an angel?' 'An angel,' says I, 'No. What makes you think that?' 'Oh, nuthing', she replied, 'nuthing . . . . it was just mummy sayin' last nicht that she was going to be clippin' y'r wings.' I write about and enjoy trials because of the characters I have met and what they stand for. Behind the writing is a genuine interest in the further advancement of the sheepdog trials and anything in connection with keeping some of the country lore alive. Too much of it is vanishing. If trials can do anything to keep younger folk in our rural life then they have a big part to play in the future."

It's a dogs life in a byre
When you're only twelve weeks old,
It's a dogs life in a byre
When the bedding's wet and cold.

It's a dogs life when you're growing
And the joys of spring aren't yours,
'Cause all the joys you ever see
Art twixt the byre doors.

And even on your birthday
When you want to bounce and play,
The same four walls are all you see
'Cause in the byre you stay.

And when you're mind is going
From confinement long and slow,
You're dragged out on a piece of rope
To see if you will show.

You see the sheep run past you,
And dying for a chase,
You run amock among them
And get a stick across the face.

They think they're very patient
And suffer long with you,
If only they could understand
The patience that you knew.